NORTHERN APPALACHIA REVIEW

VOLUME 1

CATAMOUNT
PRESS

an imprint of Sunbury Press, Inc.
Mechanicsburg, PA USA

CATAMOUNT
PRESS

an imprint of Sunbury Press, Inc.
Mechanicsburg, PA USA

For information about special discounts for bulk purchases, please contact Sunbury Press Orders Dept. at (855) 338-8359 or orders@sunburypress.com.

To request one of our authors for speaking engagements or book signings, please contact Sunbury Press Publicity Dept. at publicity@sunburypress.com.

FIRST CATAMOUNT PRESS EDITION: September 2020

Set in Adobe Garamond | Interior design by Crystal Devine.

Publisher's Cataloging-in-Publication Data
Names: PJ Piccirillo, et al.
Title: Northern appalachia review volume 1.
Description: First trade paperback edition. | Mechanicsburg, PA : Catamount Press, 2020.
Summary: An academic literary journal focused on writers from the northern appalachia region.
Identifiers: ISBN: 978-1-620062-83-8 (softcover).
Subjects: FICTION / Anthologies | LITERARY COLLECTIONS / American / General | FICTION / Cultural Heritage.

Product of the United States of America
0 1 1 2 3 5 8 13 21 34 55

Continue the Enlightenment!

Northern Appalachia Review

The Northern Appalachia Review publishes once annually. U.S. subscription rate is $19.95 for one copy. Send submissions to Editor, submissions@northernappalachiareview.com. See guidelines at northernappalachiareview.com. Address all other correspondence to The Editors, NorthernAppalachiaReview@gmail.com.

CONTENTS

INTRODUCTION

Writers tend to deal in a currency of negatives. Negative space. The old "less is more." Obsessions over the invisible part of an iceberg.

To us, nothing is something.

That's how I think of this business of understanding northern Appalachia and its literature. Attempts to define what the region *is* typically involve what it *isn't*. It's not textbook Appalachia: too industrial. You can't put a finger on its ethnic constitution. The accents are inconsistent, even within communities. The winters are cold—well, not *Vermont* cold—and while the summers are sultry, they're not the hot of Georgia. The place isn't New England, certainly not the south, not midwest, and not east coast. We're told at times we're not even Appalachia.

Talk about an identity crisis, talk about orphans.

This identity thing puts me in mind of a place in northern Pennsylvania that holds a distinction of sorts. Its chamber of commerce lays claim to occupying the only county in America where all these resources intersect: oil, coal, natural gas, iron ore, limestone, and hardwoods.

You'd think all that raw material would make it a land of wealth. But of course, it isn't, which is strange and ironic to those who don't come from places like it. The people of Appalachia, however—whether in this part with its black forests, mill towns, and muddy waters, or that part where you can get a good plate of catfish and not argue about how to pronounce Appalachia—they all get it. They've lived it. And so, one place, despite having two disparate parts, can contain commonality.

Speaking of irony, which is another currency writers like to trade in, if you couple it with drama, you have great literature. Irony and drama are rife in the northern Appalachia landscape and human experience. Such a disposition anywhere would earn its own canon, maybe the wing of some big building on a prestigious university campus. Anywhere, that is, except here. Somehow, we've been missed.

Not for long. Within these pages are the utterances of a rising collective voice. People in or of these parts have great stories to tell, and the world wants and needs to hear them.

A nascent publication dedicated as it is to a region uncharted in the universe of literature should have a fresh approach. My goal for this issue was that it come to you as much the art of the editor as of the edited. Consequently, each genre editor introduces and presents his or her chosen work as a body, arranged in concert with our mission of discovering and conveying through art who we orphans are.

I envisioned this process in respect of our contributors, too. While an exhilarating experience, having work accepted in a literary review is as well lonely. We writers wonder about the cogitations of the anonymous midwife who selects our prose or poems. What was the aesthetic, the selection criteria?

Speaking of our process, I'd like you to know about the *Northern Appalachia Review's* cover art. We knew we wanted an image that, like our content, helps make sense of this region as both distinct from and part of greater Appalachia. So it was important that the very method of selection be conscious of this place. Our editors, in a kind of contest, looked for and solicited work from visual artists across the region. We then voted on the nominations, with an eye toward a piece that spoke to the character of Northern Appalachia. In the kind of strange and beautiful circle that often comes around in art, we found that the chosen entry had been inspired by a poem. That poem, "Still Life, Ohio Valley," had been written by Scott Hanna, our poetry editor.

I've always felt that the trajectory of a work of literature continues far beyond the muzzle of the creator's wits. The words, once set on the page, belong to the reader, where, cerebrally and emotionally, they range the soul to a distance and depth proportionate to the love and sweat put into measuring just the right powder charge. While the works to follow are now yours, we hope that, together, we have planted the seeds of a literary movement.

—PJ Piccirillo, Founding Editor and Editor-in-Chief

FICTION

M aking meaning using nothing but words affixed to paper can both demand and engender a particular brand of solipsism. For this reason, among others, the act of writing is a famously solitary one. Putting together a literary journal is a fundamentally communal effort. I was very pleased to see a host of gifted writers from across the region trust us with their stories. I am excited that we're able to bring you work from the likes of Joseph Bathanti and Margo Orlando Littell, voices that represent the northern part of Appalachia on the national stage. But in another way, I am equally pleased that their work is appearing next to that of several of the region's emerging authors. I am particularly pleased that the journal is bringing readers the work of Donna Dzurilla—her deep involvement with the region and her understanding of it are *sui generis*—and that we are bringing you the first published story from Michael Lockett. We're also delivering a piece from Alison Jaenicke that offers readers the deep and immersive pleasures of the long story. Furthermore, it has also been my particular delight to work with the group of readers who came together to select the fiction for this new journal. Talking with them about the craft of fiction and how authors shape stories was, for me, the highlight of the issue.

—Damian Dressick, Fiction Editor

Northern Appalachia Review – Fiction

Acid

by Joseph Bathanti

Keith Gentile and I are thumbing into Wheeling from California, PA, a little coal-mining town along the grimy Monongahela River—Keith, among other things, is flunking out of a little college there—when a big white Ford Econoline van slows, coasts past us, and parks fifty yards up the washed-out shoulder. It's been raining with plague vengeance after a week of blizzards. We sprint after it. Fenders of water part as we run. A side door swings open, and we roll into the van. No seats. Carpet covers the floor. Nice and warm, lit votive candles stationed here and there.

Keith and I feel lucky to have copped a ride in this monsoon. But the occupants of the van are midgets. Like the guys on *Studio Wrestling*. Blocky and muscular, a set of pecs on a belt buckle. Long hair and beards. I've never met one, and I know Keith hasn't either.

Nobody but the driver, Mack, really speaks at first: the usual *where you from, where you headed?* The van is rigged to accommodate his stature: a big high seat, so he can peer over the dashboard, brake, and throttle on an elevated platform his feet can reach. Marty, the guy riding shotgun, turns and looks at us the whole time. Everyone else—all midgets—sitting or lying on the floor, nod in greeting. Very serious, but friendly enough. Some sleep. A few get up and walk around. They're short enough to not ding their heads on the van's ceiling.

There was a time when Keith and I would have cracked up, laughed like little kids in church. We have long careers in undistinguished behavior. *A van full of midgets. C'mon!* But tonight there's no laugh in us. We're glad to have landed in such a mellow space on such a bad night—and Keith, who can be like some wild animal out there, needs to be handled with kid gloves.

Mack says they're headed for Wheeling too. Asks if we know where the whorehouses are. Neither Keith nor I have ever been to a whorehouse. Back in high school, not that long ago at all—last year—we tagged along with some other guys and got as far as the parlor in a whorehouse underneath the Homestead High Level Bridge. Then we chickened out. Marty says there's supposed to be one in Wheeling where the girls are all dwarves, no shit. That's the one they're looking for. I think he's goofing around, so I just laugh.

"Square business," Marty says. "I'm not kidding."

"Maybe you'd like to have a go with a dwarf," Mack suggests.

Keith tells him he's engaged, so he can't have a go with anybody. His girl, back in Pittsburgh, is pregnant, and he plans to marry her.

"How about you, then?" Marty nods toward me. "You up for that Wheeling feeling?"

I tell him I don't know, but of course, I have no interest in such a thing. He and Mack laugh.

Then, like they're reading my mind, they give a spiel about the differences between midgets and dwarves. Midgets are simply miniature versions of regular people. It's a matter of proportions. Midgets are scaled-down homo sapiens, like someone bathed them in the shrink ray. Dwarves, on the other hand, possess abnormal body proportions: biggish heads, truncated limbs. They're skilled artificers and craftsmen, noted for legendary strength. Mack and Marty want to make sure that we know we're in a van full of dwarves—not midgets.

"Mack can lift a Shetland pony," Marty confides. Mack confirms this with a sober nod. "The actual munchkins in *The Wizard of Oz*. Some are dwarves, some midgets. Check it out next time it's on."

They're dressed in normal clothes, but I keep picturing them in chain mail, little broadswords, and helmets, like Gimli and Ori and Nori and the rest of them in *The Hobbit*. I'm worried I'm going to start laughing, and what's more, I literally feel Keith sending out his signature shrill vibe. He's struggling mightily to not let go with a frantic laughing jag—which would turn into some freak-out requiring hospitalization. But then we both calm down, and through telepathic powers old friends possess—we were born nearly the same minute at Pittsburgh Hospital—agree not to look at each other.

It's late, the early hours of the morning, rain pounding down on the road's omniscient hush. The dwarves bed down, blow out all but one candle. Mack and Marty, turned to the road for the duration, pop into the tape deck something I don't recognize. It might be chanting. Medieval woodwinds. It's nice and warm in the van and the music's very soothing. Keith and I, completely soaked, settle into a pile of blankets in a corner of the van. The others sleep. They snore like it's scripted, and their beards luff up in the wind-drift of their heavy exhales like the dwarves in *Snow White*.

I think we pass into West Virginia—Keith and I are going to celebrate a little down there, get his mind off things—the legal drinking age is eighteen—when my head knocks off something as I angle into those blankets. It feels like steel, so I pull back the blanket. There's just this last tiny flame on the white votive wick. But I know what a gun looks like. Not just one, but more and more as I inch back the blankets: shotguns and machine guns and pistols. An entire arsenal. Dope too. Bricks and bricks of Mary Jane and countless big clear baggies of white powder. I decide not to wake Keith, but he's right there at my elbow gaping.

"Jesus Christ, Fritzy," he hisses. "Jesus Christ."

Keith is not a murderer, but he could reach for a gun. I cover the stuff back up and whisper, "Just keep cool. Okay?"

"Keep cool," he mutters. "Keep cool. Keep cool." He lies back down and pulls a blanket over his head, reciting, "Keep cool." The blanket pulses with his inevitable detonation.

From the tape deck, flutes rustle like wind. Our tires slish across the deserted highway. The barely guttering candle flame solemnly laps the glass it sits in. The dwarves slumber. Dangerously sad. Like all has been lost. Mythic. These guys are from another world. They have guns, and they're running dope, and it's up to me to do something about it—to save Keith and me. To save the world. But I don't know what to do, and I'm not even sure what side I'm on.

There's an explosion, and the dwarves come out of their blankets. Like Judgment Day. As if they have the drill down pat. Keith sits up—like in a Poe story. Someone has dropped a bomb on us or maybe broadsided us with a bazooka. Mack fights the wheel. We're going sideways. Marty's yelling, "Jesus Christ, hold on." The van convulses. There's the decided stench of incineration. In a twirl, we may be on fire.

The dwarves keen like a Greek chorus. Like the explosion was their cue. Like they know exactly what's happening—what's hit us: what they've expected all along. The stakes are that high: the guns and dope. It all comes clear in that instant—that they're part of something. Keith hasn't moved. Just sits there like rigor mortis as we spin and spin off the road into oblivion.

Mack gets us to the shoulder. Marty turns and says, "It's a blowout. Front right tire." But the dwarves screech so loudly, they don't hear. At that moment, out of quite literally nowhere, the very ether, a Pennsylvania Highway Patrolman pulls up behind us, red and blue hazards flailing. We've traveled miles, through farmland and spooky woods, on a road flat and straight as perdition: no entrance; above all, no exit. Keith quickens. He's coming back to life. Through the van's rear window, I watch the trooper walk through the rain toward us—coming into relief, bigger and bigger, against the sodden dawn. The keen of the dwarves is suicidal.

"Shut the fuck up," Mack screams at his buddies. And suddenly there is absolute silence, as the trooper reaches Mack's open window, takes one look at him, then switches on a gargantuan flashlight and peers into the back of the van.

With that searchlight in my eyes, I can't see a thing, but I chance a look at Keith. He smiles; his mouth unseals. Then he laughs. Louder and louder, demonically, like he's finally gone over: knocking up Bonnie, flunking out, the dwarves, and the guns and dope, the blown tire and now the law. Sometimes, it's too fucking much.

The trooper digs his light into Keith, bathing him in technicolor caricature. Keith, like a crazy-ass super villain experiencing some kind of fanatic conversion, stumbling upon what it's really all about. Like Saint Paul: transmission zapped, electrical system exponentially shorted. Right there: Keith snaps, and I witness it. It's all I can do to hang on myself.

That long cone of the trooper's white light. Keith swallows it – the light itself, that abyss of concentrated incandescence. Scarfs the entire scene—like it's his last meal. Down his throat, in the caverns of his guts, dwarves caper toward their weapons. Votive fires ignite. Sirens lift from the land, a regiment of hallucinatory lights on the backs of state cruisers arrived to shoot it out with us. I see the whole world inside Keith. Entire armies march.

More Than an Accident

by Michael Lockett

Though my mom told me not to, I leaned into old cousin Walter. He was looking through a magnifying glass at the photo of the accident on the front page of the paper. I had seen it three times already: the charred-out cab of Uncle Butch's truck turned-around on the railroad tracks with the front of the train engine embedded in its side. With the magnifying glass, I could see Uncle Butch's skull, leaning cockeyed over the middle of the seat.

I listened as people talked about the accident. The overgrown brush at the railroad crossing. The force of the train dragging the truck some five-hundred-feet. The explosion, they said, knocked the engine from the track.

My mother motioned for me to sit beside her in one of the folding chairs in the funeral parlor. Miss Lorraine sat in the row ahead of us. Turned around, Miss Lorraine said I looked just like Uncle Butch and my dad when they were kids.

I looked towards my grandparents and my dad, where they sat in the front row of chairs. The back of my father's arm rested on the empty chair beside him. In the front of the room, surrounded by blue flowers my mother called carnations, sat Uncle Butch in a small, white urn. I wondered how they'd fit his tall body in such a small thing. He had lived on endless packages of bologna, so maybe he'd been extra flammable.

"What do you remember most about your uncle?" Miss Lorraine asked me.

I think she saw how the urn caught my attention. Her face moved into my view like the moon in the night sky as she leaned toward me. I could smell her perfume, something like flowers. I counted the lines around her eyes through her rose-colored glasses as she forced a smile.

His goat Lucifer, I spouted-off, not really thinking it through.

Miss Lorraine chuckled.

"You had about thirty seconds to get from the car to Butch's trailer door before Lucifer was bucking at your rear," Mom said. "That goat and Butch were a lot alike."

At the front of the parlor, Aunt May caught my attention as she crossed the urn and turned to my grandparents and my dad. She wore a long black dress that reached the floor and a covering on top of her head. She was old-time Pentecost, mom always said, a photograph come-to-life. She stood over my father and grandparents, linking hands with them and praying in tongues as her body swayed.

I pushed closer to my mother and held her hand as the prayer grew to a wail that hurt my ears. Mom said I had nothing to fear of the Holy Spirit, but it worried me to see folks so worked up.

My father had joined right in with Aunt May, his arm raised straight up in the air. I heard him say "Bless the Lord" before he rolled into a machine gun fire of syllables that echoed from the front of the parlor, "Kashunda-Ka-book-Kashunda—"

Because father was a minister, Uncle Butch called him Reverend Ike, after the preacher from the radio. Mom said this wasn't nice because Reverend Ike was a crook.

As Aunt May's prayer wound down, a hush fell over the room. I thought more about Miss Lorraine's question.

I remembered most the one day we were at Uncle Butch's trailer, and he asked mom why she had bruises on her neck. I remembered watching from the screen door while Uncle Butch and my dad went rounds in the yard as Lucifer sprinted around them making terrible bleating noises.

Uncle Butch gave my dad a bloody nose.

"I was at that tent revival, up Moss Creek," Miss Lorraine said, breaking my thoughts. She turned her face to my mother.

"Butch was cutting-up in his seat. Reverend Hugill stopped the song service and called him to the altar in front of everyone and said, 'Young man if you don't stop playing games with God, you'll die a fiery death!' Butch walked out. Never stepped foot in a church again."

Both mom and Miss Lorraine dropped their heads.

"After that night, Butch went AWOL from the army," Mom said. She picked up where Miss Lorraine left off. "He'd freeze to death before he'd allow a kerosene heater in that old trailer of his. Never settled down. Never kept a job. I think it drove him to drink."

Mom and Miss Lorraine turned their heads in opposite directions.

I realized I hadn't considered what happened to Uncle Butch to be more than an accident. I had just been listening to cousin Walter and the others. I slid my hand across Mom's sleeve. Where it drew up, I noticed bruises. Mother was quick to pull it back down.

"What does it mean to play games with God," I asked my mom.

"The Bible says, better to be cold or hot. If you are lukewarm, God will spit you out of his mouth. It means *you* choose good or bad. Nothing between."

Her words confused me. I never thought of Uncle Butch as bad, and when he cuffed-up my dad in the yard that day, I found him to be downright good. My father stood behind a pulpit, but he did badly. It seemed as I looked around the room, I could list the good and bad in all—even in myself for disobeying my mom. I kept thinking about the photo of the accident.

Reverend Hugill came to the funeral and gave a sermon standing by Uncle Butch's urn. He was a big man with white hair in a black suit. When he spoke, his voice was so deep that I felt it in my chest. It silenced the room. I feared he'd call us up one-by-one and give us each our due warning.

"We have a choice," he said. "Which road will you take?"

Reverend Hugill's words filled me with fear as he warned about playing games with God, lest we end up like my Uncle Butch.

When everyone stepped outside the funeral home, I stood between my parents. I heard the rumble of a jet and spotted a trail of white dust in the sky. I held tightly to my mother's hand. I saw the jet bursting into flames overhead and crashing down on us because people had played games with God.

I reckoned, in the newspaper photo of this accident, someone would find my skull with a clouded magnifying glass. It would be there in the heap of the funeral home's wreckage, cratered into the ground, black smoke rolling upward.

Row Twelve

by Donna Dzurilla

The front doors of the unemployment office wouldn't open for another fifteen minutes. I was twenty-fifth in a line that wrapped around the white brick one-story office building. I could see the front door from my vantage point, and like the rest of the people around me, I could picture myself anywhere else on a sticky August morning in Pittsburgh. The number of people I knew grew smaller and smaller each week until today when I recognized no one. It wasn't just at unemployment. There were a whole lot of people I didn't see anywhere anymore. Lots of people moved south for work if they could afford it. Rather than pass legislation to indefinitely support workers who lost their jobs during the downturn of the steel industry in 1983, the government chose to extend benefits to thirty-nine weeks. At forty weeks, we were on our own.

To pass time in line, people around me drank coffee grabbed at the Stop n Go around the corner, read newspapers, or talked. Some left their spots to catch up on news or gossip with people they knew, but not before asking that their spot be saved. The air, humid and hazy, trapped cigarette smoke above our heads. I passed the time watching the smokers. I liked to guess how long each smoker was out of work by the way they finished a cigarette, careful to tamp it out and, if it had tobacco left, stick it back in the pack or a shirt pocket. Nobody wasted cigarettes. The newly unemployed, mostly young guys, finished with a quick drag, exhaling through their nose. They ground the butts into the scorching sidewalk, shredding the paper membrane away to reveal the once snowy-white round filter reduced to a sickly spray of caramel rusted tufts. Others, accustomed to the wait-then-shuffle of unemployment lines, flicked smoldering butts into the adjacent parking lot. Anger, disenchantment, and despair. All in one flick of a butt. If I were a smoker, that'd be my group.

The sound of the bottom of the plate glass and aluminum doors clacking and scraping across the concrete caused a hush to descend among the group, quickly followed by murmurs as people reclaimed their spots and pushed forward towards the door.

Voices rose, then quieted as the front of the line entered the bottle-neck of the doorway. Once inside the building, the crush of smells—lack of personal hygiene, stale beer, and cigarette smoke—made me gag and I covered my mouth and nose. After the early morning sun, I paused and squinted to adjust to the dimness of the cave-like office. It reminded me of driving into a tunnel. Everyone heading inside slowed down for no good reason, yet still found their lane.

It was like any other government office: tile floor patterned with streaks of dirt, fluorescent lights buzzing overhead, green metal desks and chairs gathered in rows on one side of the room. Orange plastic seating lined the opposite wall, and an American flag hung horizontally on the back wall, sagging a bit in the middle.

Clerks, almost exclusively middle-aged white women, manned the claim windows that ran along the center, creating rows which we queued into. The numbers one through twelve hung from placards suspended above their heads.

My social security number ended in five, which meant I reported on Fridays and because my last name started with a W I reported to row twelve. I couldn't get to the window before my assigned time of 10:30. I counted the number of people in front of me and figured each would spend about five minutes at the window. It would be close.

My first time at signing up for unemployment benefits taught me that being early at the window wasn't a good idea. Arriving early, I made it to the window at 9:30 rather than 10:30. The clerk sent me to the back of the line. I ignored the smirks, snickers, and eye rolls. They would sometimes give a few minutes leeway, but clerks didn't screw around. After nineteen weeks of signing up I knew how to time it out. If it looked like I'd reach the window before 10:30, I'd let someone behind me go first.

Out of habit I turned and checked the clock above the door. Not even 8:30 and it had to be eighty degrees already. I'd be lucky to get to the window before lunch.

An older man in a filthy Steeler t-shirt in row nine yelled, "Stan, what the hell are you doing here? I thought you'd be one of the last ones they'd let go." He motioned for me to get the attention of the man in front of me.

I hadn't seen Stan in line before. New sign-ups asked a lot of questions and slowed everything down. His hair, coal black and in need of a shampoo, hung well past his collar. His burning greens, streaked with oil and grime, smelled of gasoline. *Probably just finished changing the oil in his car, or more likely, his truck*, I thought. Foreign-made truck, I bet. He could have at least showered and put some clean clothes on.

Stan waved at the guy in the Steeler t-shirt and in a deep, low voice said, "Catch up with you later, man."

Recognition and reunions were inevitable. I heard plans made weekly for coffee, lunch, or a couple beers. Mostly just a couple of beers back at the union hall. Men who defined themselves as steelworkers hadn't yet given up on returning to their jobs. Keeping up with each other, looking for news about orders and what management was up to helped them hold onto their hopes of being called back to work, and more importantly, to hold onto their dwindling sense of self.

"You," the big-haired polyester clad woman garnered everyone's attention as she motioned to a twenty-year-old kid at the head of my row.

A blue bandana stuck out of the back pocket of his jeans and the Levi jean's jacket he wore looked new. The sound in the room gradually rose again and I watched the back of his head bob as he spoke to the clerk. He'd have to answer the three questions, the same three everyone answers to collect a benefit check.

"Were you able and available for work?"

"Did you work, and if so, do you have earnings to report?"

"Have you registered for JobCorp?"

Only complete idiots say no to the first and last question. Honesty wasn't appreciated by the government. Neither was a complete idiot.

The clerk's voice cleared the low hum of conversation. "I don't want to hear about your sister in Ohio. They got movers in Ohio. I'll take that as a no. You weren't available for work."

She pointed to the orange plastic chairs along the wall and told him to sit. He started to argue and when the clerk pointed to the chairs a second time, he lost his temper and slammed his hand into the wall next to the window just above where she sat. She stood up and backed away from the window.

"What's going on?" The guard from the door met the kid by the window. "C'mon, don't cause any trouble. Listen to the lady. Sit."

It would be late afternoon before the kid would be called to one of the green pleather-clad chairs to explain to the man at the desk why he was unavailable for work, and learn, as such, that he wouldn't receive a check for the week.

As the line settled into the rhythm of the unemployed versus the clerks, I looked around to pass the time. More than a window separated the clerks from us. The clerks sat in judgement of us, the unemployed. None of the clerks looked like they needed a bath or nursed a hangover. They had the dignity of a job and sat tall. We stood and shuffled along. The men in line outnumbered the women two to one.

Most of the women were dressed like me: cotton t-shirt that clung to a sweaty back, jeans, and sandals. One, most likely headed for a job interview after signing up, wore a padded-shoulder business suit with a bow-tie blouse and pumps. I wondered what kind of place was hiring women in suits. Bank, probably, but having to wear pantyhose, in this heat?

A lot of the girls I graduated from high school with wanted a job where they could wear a suit and heels. I couldn't imagine being trapped in an outfit like that. I came home dirty from the mill, but the dust and dirt meant that I put in a solid day's work. Working as an electrician and in maintenance was better than shoveling ore in the stock house next to the heat of the furnace. I spent most of my time in the pipe shop or powerhouse climbing with the wire gang. I'm not the kind of woman made to sit behind a desk or counter all day.

Three women balanced children on their hips while waiting to sign up. When I first started signing up, they let strollers in. They changed it because they said strollers took up too much space. I think it had more to do with attitudes about mothers who worked, like they shouldn't work and if they hadn't been working there'd be ample work for the guys in line. Everybody had someone to blame for layoffs. I tended towards blaming workers who bought pickup trucks made by foreign companies with foreign-made steel. I believe that helped put me in row twelve for God-knows-how-many weeks.

The woman closest to me struggled with her little boy. He was cute—blond ringlets, blue eyes and wore a Pirates shirt and shorts. She kept a tight hold as the toddler squirmed and fussed in her arms until she tired of the struggle and endless wait. She put him down to let him stand. They began a tight dance, the little boy twisting in circles as his mother tried to keep a grasp on his forearm and trying to avoid him colliding into someone. The boy broke away by reversing direction, only to stop and fling himself onto the floor, crying. The floor was filthy. Mopping from the night before left zig-zagged lines of dirt dragged across the length of the tile.

"Get up off that floor." She grabbed him by the hand and pulled him up. He broke away for a second, but as she grabbed the back of his other wrist, he swung around and clipped his mother in the face. She reacted without thought and raised her hand to strike him but caught herself. She pulled him close and he clung to her leg.

A man's voice boomed out from across the room, "Go ahead; smack him. Kid needs his ass whipped."

The child's mother drew in her breath and redness swept from the base of her neck up to her forehead. She turned to see who made the comment. The rows quieted for a moment but quickly filled with murmured judgments about her ability to parent.

I looked away, not wanting to add to her embarrassment or shame.

An older woman who stood in the row next to me heckled the mother's harasser. "You got a lot of nerve, Ed. Mind your own god-damned business. You wouldn't know what to do with a kid. You can't keep a wife. Leave the poor woman alone."

All eyes in the room turned towards the loudmouth, who we all now knew as Ed, and waited for his response.

The security guard again intervened and walked in Ed's general direction. "Is there a problem?" he asked.

"No problem," said Ed. "Why do you care anyway? Unemployment cop. What are you anyway? Something between a fish cop and a mall cop?"

"Probably closer to a fish cop, you know, as I police the wildlife, smart ass. You want to start all over? Maybe I'll just throw your ass out and you'll lose two weeks' worth of checks. How about you minding your own business and keeping your mouth shut?"

The little boy pulled away from his mother and plopped down onto the dirty floor. His mother reached down and scooped him up. Without meeting anyone's eyes, she hurried towards the door. People separated to let her through, then turned back to face the clerks at the windows.

I silently urged the clerk on through the rest of the morning until finally the greasy-haired welder in front of me made it to the window. It was 11:58 when I reached the clerk. I'd seen clerks shut windows in people's faces when the clock hands hit noon. Anyone left in line had to leave the building and get back in line after 1:00 when the clerks returned from lunch. The partitions around me shook as clerks on either side closed their windows, ignoring anyone who remained in line. The people behind me turned and headed to the door, resigned to a long, hot afternoon.

A stack of manilla folders sat on the low file cabinet to the right of the clerk. A loud silkscreen print of yellow, pink, and purple bouquets blossomed up and around her double D breasts. Dry, tired-looking blonde hair stood teased up in front, stiffened with layers of hairspray to form a wall separating her bangs from the rest of her head. A pristine copy of *A Duke in Danger: A Barbara Cartland Romance* lay on top of another low metal file cabinet behind her. A half-full mug of coffee with clots of creamer clumps floating on top sat on her narrow desktop. I handed the clerk my benefits card, a small rectangular card made of oak tag folded in half, filled on one side with stamped dates and signatures.

"Got your social security card?" she asked without looking up at me.

"Yes, ma'am. Here."

The clerk checked it against the signature on the benefits card then the one in my file folder. Satisfied my identification was in order, the clerk rattled off the three questions that I knew by heart, without waiting for my answer.

"Yes, no, yes,'" I said, matching her tone and tempo. I didn't mean to. It just happened.

The clerk glared up at me and asked, "Are you mocking me?"

Without waiting for a reply, the clerk stamped two dates and initialed the card. She handed the dog-eared card back to me and spoke to me in a way that removed any doubt as to further conversation. "Sign here and here. Don't lose your card. Be back in two weeks unless you get a call-back. If you get called back to work, call the number on the front of the card and report your return to work date."

I signed twice, once for each week where the clerk indicated and then thanked her for working into her lunch hour.

I stuck my sosh and benefits cards in my wallet and made my way towards the guard who nodded as I met him at the door. He unlocked it, let me out, then locked up again. I walked right smack into Stan, the guy from the line. I managed to knock him off balance a little.

"You're from Duquesne Works, aren't you?" he asked. "I seen you around. Got time for a cup of coffee?"

"Watch it," I said as I instinctively pulled my purse closer and backed up. I didn't want to pick up any oil stains on my jeans and t-shirt.

"Hey, stop," he called as he followed me, "you ran into me. I mean, hold on, I was waiting for you. I'm Stan, Stan Krawczyk. You're Duquesne Works? Maintenance, right? I was in front of you in line today. I seen you around before though. Got time for a cup of coffee?"

I could use a cup of coffee after standing in line all morning, but already had my two cups for the day. Stan, from in-front-of-me-in-line, had a wedding ring on and hadn't bothered to clean up before coming to the unemployment office. I hope he didn't think that just because I was laid off it meant that I was looking for someone to fill my time. I wanted to get home and take David bike riding. It was already scorching hot, but I'd promised him before I left the house.

"Look," I lied, "I'm seeing someone—and I don't date married men or date guys from the mill."

"Oh no, I didn't mean like that. I'm not married. I mean I'm widowed." He twisted his wedding ring. "I don't date. I mean I'm not dating yet. That wasn't me asking you out."

"Really, then what?" He offended me a little. He threw in the widower remark and it made me start to feel sorry for him. Maybe that was his hook. I mean, I wasn't someone to ask out for coffee? I wasn't beautiful, I would do as a woman, something, to look at across a cup of coffee. "I don't mix work and my social life, okay?"

On the unemployment line, just like punching out at quitting time, I was just one of the guys. I kept that mindset. Last thing I needed was an unemployed boyfriend. Once guys heard I was an electrician, they seemed to only talk about how I "made good money." What they didn't think or know was that I was raising a kid on my own and that yeah, I made "good money," but I always knew that layoffs occurred periodically and were always a possibility that my "good money" had to cover. "Good money" ended up being just enough money.

Stan's voice broke through my train of thought.

"This ain't social. It's union-related business. You got me all wrong. I mean you're attractive and all but you ain't my type. Look, you and me, we started out on the wrong foot here. We're trying to get a bunch of the Duquesne Works guys—ahhh—I mean workers, together and meet."

Stan raised his hand to stop any protests that I might interrupt him with. "Just hear me out. I know you ain't a steelworker. You're out of maintenance, electrician, right? Grievance man's assistant for the electrical union someone told me. I don't know what to call you—you're still a journeyman, right?"

"Journeyman, my ass," I snapped. "I earned my certification years ago. I'm a master electrician."

"I don't know what the electrical union is doing for you guys, but our national ain't doing shit. Our local president called the national office and told them about management, U.S. Steel management, trying to sneak equipment out of Duquesne Works late one-night last week. We're trying to get as many guys—ahhh—union workers, together as we can. We gotta take care of ourselves if the union won't."

I chose my next words carefully. "Stan, it's nice to meet you and my name's Louise. Look, this puts me in a tough spot. You know a grievance man is considered a local union official, right? I might just be an assistant because of how many guys we have, but I was elected to represent the local members of the International Brotherhood of Electrical Workers, not the whole goddamned yard. I have to think this over."

"We don't want you there as a grievance man, assistant, whatever. I was thinking we could use you cause you're a woman. We need some-body to talk to the other women and the secretaries, and stuff. We need as much help as we can get."

He clearly had no sense that he was pissing me off. It didn't matter that it wasn't his intent. I tried to let it go but couldn't.

"Why can't you talk to the women yourselves? Maybe it's all the bullshit you guys dished out over the years? Nobody wants to talk to you? You know, I had to be twice as good as guys I trained with, just to end up at the same pay rate. I climbed all over that mill, to all the places guys wouldn't fit or didn't want to go. I never refused any job given me, even if I dragged myself home, tired as hell. They sent me places a man would never go, just because they could. You know what? I went. They waited for me to quit. I didn't."

I felt sweat trickling down my spine. It was probably leaving a mark through my t-shirt.

"I ain't one of them guys. I supported you women when you wanted your own showers and your own toilets. Not all the guys did. If you're worried about representation, we have the union presidents coming to the meeting. We really need you to talk to the secretaries and office clerks. They work directly with management. If they could get us information about what management was planning . . ."

"You gotta be kidding. I gotta talk to secretaries? They don't invite me to their Tupperware parties, okay? Most think of me as competition or as a poor, white trash divorcee that they don't want to associate with. I mean, please, like I want one of their husbands. Why aren't you just asking their boyfriends or husbands to ask them? The office girls aren't brilliant, but they're smart. You want them to lose their jobs? Most of the guys they are married to or dating are laid off."

I was really losing patience, and the humidity and sun bouncing off the sidewalk were getting to me. "Look, I'm going to pass out from heat exhaustion. Forget coffee. I'll come to your meeting if I can get a babysitter. When and where?"

Before he could answer, the lock on the office door opened.

"Fish cop," Ed, the ignoramus, said to the guard while leaving the office.

"Whoa, Stan," Ed bellowed, "finally breaking that dry spell?" He pushed out his chest and beer belly as he waddled towards us.

I don't know which plant Ed worked out of, but he sure knew a lot of people. More than likely, a lot of people knew of him. He hadn't impressed me with his earlier performance humiliating the poor woman trying to control her tired toddler. She probably missed signing up for her two weeks of checks because she had to leave.

"Stan, it's about time," he went on, "you relieve some of that sexual tension. Might improve that gloomy disposition of yours. Lighten you up a bit, Mr. Gloom and Doom."

"Ed, knock it off. We're talking union business."

Ed positioned himself between me and Stan. I could smell the whiskey on him. "Union business, huh?' he said. "When did you join the International Brotherhood of Electrical Workers, Stan?"

I wasn't going to stand for any crap from him. I didn't know him, and I didn't want to be seen with him. That he knew I was single, and an electrician, was downright creepy.

I spoke up. "Wow. Impressive, you know what IBEW stands for and you're not even an electrician, are you, Ed? You look like a crane operator to me." I looked pointedly at his beer belly.

Ed couldn't keep his mouth shut. "Last I heard IBEW stood for Infernal Bi—"

I cut him off. "Big man, aren't you? You're nothing but a bully. Did you ever consider that lady with the kid couldn't afford a sitter? That maybe she hated bringing her kid here?"

"Maybe she should have thought of that before pushing a kid out."

Stan put his hand on Ed's chest to stop him. "Stop. You insulted enough ladies today. Get the hell out of here, Ed. Go home and sober up."

I had enough. "I have to pick my son up at the sitter," I lied.

"Bye-bye, Lou-Lou. You be sweet to Stan you hear?" Ed began to sing, "Lou-Lou had a boyfriend, her boyfriend had a truck, Lou-Lou liked to shift the gears, her boyfriend liked to—"

"Go fuck yourself, Ed. You think I never heard that one before?" I glared at Stan. "Nice company you keep. Original songwriter." I turned and began to walk away. Ed knew my name. Great. It was impossible to be a woman working in the mill and remain anonymous. I'd been rushed and cornered a couple times until guys learned not to mess with me. I heard about the bets they made. No one would ever win betting on me. I worked hard a lot of years to get certified and build my seniority up enough to not get bumped from the day shift. Dating or sleeping with someone I worked with wasn't going to screw it up. That and crying at work, letting them see you cry, were things a woman couldn't come back from.

I heard Stan saying, "He's not my friend." I continued walking but looked back.

"Ed, get out of here before I lose my temper." Ed pulled out and lit a cigarette and walked back past the door of the office.

"Hey," Stan raised his right hand to stop me or maybe say goodbye. "I'm not like him and he isn't my friend. I'm sorry. You shouldn't have to listen to that crap. That meeting, the one I was talking about, is at Huckster's Bar, back room, tomorrow night around seven."

Over my shoulder I said, "I'll see what I can do." I pulled on the hem of my t-shirt and wiggled it away from my stomach and sweaty back. I searched the parking lot and found my Ford Escort at the end of the first row, the row furthest away from the unemployment office.

It made sense what Stan said. We probably would need to pull everyone together to stop U.S. Steel from shutting us down. It was happening up and down the valley. It'd be a long shot though. We couldn't get our members to agree to a decent contract on the first go-round of votes.

Stan was sincere. He seemed like a decent guy. I decided to go to the meeting.

I had nothing left to lose.

This I Know

by Margo Orlando Littell

The ground had thawed. In the air was the warm fizz of early spring, which whisked away the protective coziness of houses that had been shut up tight for months. People opened front doors, raised the storm windows. They wanted to be outside now, in the sun, their dry winter feet in sneakers that slipped on the damp earth.

It was Stella who suggested they hike to the cross at Jumonville. Ramsy hadn't been there in years, not since his first year in Shelk, when he grew curious about the cross after spotting it from the highway each time he drove out to the Rural King. Sixty feet tall, the steel cross had been built high on Dunbar's Knob in the Appalachian Mountains, marking a battle site from the French and Indian War. Too many ghosts for Ramsy's taste, too much distant death. Besides, he wasn't one for hiking, and preferred to spend early spring days cleaning dead leaves from his house's gutters. Still, he said yes to Stella. So little made her happy. She'd been grieving her kidnapped baby, Lucy, a year now; Ramsy thought it no small miracle that she'd made it to another spring.

He parked his truck at the base of the trail, and together they began walking. Stella wore only a crocheted shawl, and Ramsy soon unbuttoned his flannel coat. The grade was steep, and the exertion made it hard to breathe. Ramsy's thighs ached, a reminder of how little he'd moved during the winter. His life was sitting and driving or pouring beers behind his bar.

They paused for several minutes when they emerged into an open area with stone benches surrounding an old hewn podium. "Seth and I got married here," Stella said quietly. "It's called the Green Cathedral. We wound strands of lights in the trees."

Ramsy's gut twisted. "You never told me that."

"It doesn't matter now, after what he did."

"Still, being back here—"

"He took enough from me. He can't take this mountain, too."

This soon after winter, it seemed a ruined place. Rotting leaves floated in the murky water of a dormant font, and the litter the snow had concealed now dotted the ground. But in the crescent of grass around the podium, daffodils and crocuses were just pushing into bud. "It's beautiful, isn't it?" Stella said. She surprised Ramsy by making the Sign of the Cross. He'd never known her to be a churchgoer, though he'd suggested it after Lucy disappeared—awkwardly, with no real belief it would do any good at all. She'd told him then how the dry coughs and boredly rustling hymnals left her cold. But maybe something had changed; maybe faith was sliding into the space that hope once filled.

"Should we keep walking?" Ramsy said, and Stella nodded. They were near the top now. Soon they'd be able to see fifty miles to the horizon, across three states and seven counties. Ramsy knew there to be relief in altitude, as though some weight lifted from the shoulders when you looked out over the world below. Everything so far, so small.

There it was, just ahead: the cross. Ramsy saw now they weren't alone. Children from the Christian school at the base of the hill were sitting in rows under near-blooming pink dogwoods, listening to a Bible story being read from a book. In the grass around them, and at the edges of the forest beside the trail, were bright plastic Easter eggs. Pink, purple, green, yellow, orange, tucked behind rocks and scattered among the ferns. Suddenly the children jumped up and began to run, sprinting toward the eggs they'd spotted as their teacher read.

Ramsy and Stella stepped off the trail, careful not to trample any eggs. The children screamed and laughed and scooped eggs from the ground, dropping them into plastic bags looped over their wrists. Stella bent down and picked up an egg by her foot. It had split apart and spilled jellybeans into the dirt, but Stella brushed them off and snapped the halves of the egg back together. Beside them, a little girl appeared, and Stella tilted the egg into her tiny waiting hands.

The hunt was over in minutes. The children grouped together once more beneath the dogwood, their mouths full of candy, and then the teacher stood, and they began to sing a hymn. *Jesus loves me! This I know, for the Bible tells me so. Little ones to Him belong; they are weak, but He is strong. Yes, Jesus loves me! Yes, Jesus loves me! Yes, Jesus loves me! The Bible tells me so.* Then the children lined up and streamed past Ramsy and Stella, chattering excitedly, clutching their egg-filled bags to their spring-coated chests.

Now Ramsy and Stella were alone at the cross. Ramsy followed Stella across the grassy clearing and looked up. The sky was so white that the cross, if he squinted, could almost be mistaken for a cloud. A low wire barrier was strung around the cross, but Stella stepped over it and pressed her hands against the cold steel. Ramsy turned away. He looked down at the towns spread below him, Shelk to the east, Moon Run a bit to the west of that, Four Points just another clutch of bare trees to the north. The view was a prickly quilt of black branches, empty roads, and patches of white where, in the summer, farmers grew modest crops of corn and soybeans and hay. Somewhere out there, in the swelling ground around Shelk, was where Lucy disappeared.

Ten feet in front of the cross was a stone bench, and Ramsy sat down. This was where he'd pray, if he were a praying man; or maybe he'd kneel before the bench, facing the cross, thumbing to favorite verses in a well-worn Bible while the damp ground soaked his knees. But what or whom would he pray for, if that was why he'd come? Even with the cross looming at his back, he couldn't recall the words to a prayer. For a moment he wished he knew the words that Stella was praying, but he feared her prayers might be less words than keening.

He didn't look over when Stella sat beside him. In the distance they could still hear the children's laughter. "Will it always be so terrible?" Stella said quietly. She wasn't crying. She rarely did.

Ramsy said, "I don't know. But I know you won't always remember that it is."

Nothing in the white sky or bare trees or even the new-budding ferns could tell them how it would be a month from now, a year from now, their flesh warming and cooling with the seasons and Lucy still gone. The eggs, and the candy inside, made them crave something sweet. But all they could taste on the way back down the mountain was the fresh damp air, cleaned by a cold spring rain that would resurrect the withered roots beneath their feet.

Sweat Equity

by Alison Condie Jaenicke

From the gravel shoulder, I strain to spot the three guys perched on the wooded hillside below. When I slam the car door, their heads turn toward me momentarily, then turn back. The woods here are thin scribbles of new growth through which I can see the building site, rocky soil with just a start of a gray cinder block foundation. Deep Creek Lake shimmers in the far distance.

I scramble down the hill and stand near them. The old, lanky builder sits hunched over his chipped ham on Wonder Bread, knees jutting up in sharp triangles. Next to him, a chubby teenager, red-faced cherub with black curls, sprawls with his tight, muddy jeans laid out like blue sausages on the slope, crumpled brown paper bag beside him. Standing below them, a rangy twenty-something in white cleats nibbles potato chips with crooked teeth. Mr. White Cleats tells a story about how some guy stopped his big '75 Buick in the middle of the road outside of Oakland, turned off the lights, and left. The storyteller's friends, five of them in a Dodge Colt, came along and smashed into the Buick. The driver's head went through the windshield.

"Why did he do it?" I ask, meaning why would someone leave his car parked in the middle of a dark, winding country road. The old builder goes on eating, but the two younger ones look at me.

"He ain't got all his marbles," Mr. White Cleats says, like it's obvious. "He done it another time, too. This time he's drunk, but the first time he weren't." I'm not sure if he means the owner of the Buick or the Dodge, the parker or the crasher—both sound like they could use a few more marbles—but I don't want to stop him again, and deep down I know that this could easily be one of my down-on-their-luck relatives from Fayette County, whose escapades get transmitted weekly from my grandmother to my mom to me in DC—long-distance soap opera via phone line.

He goes on to describe the injuries—the long gash on the driver's face, how he was taken to the hospital in Morgantown where they fixed his damaged tear duct. How when our storyteller went to the hospital to visit, he took a side trip to the empty WVU football stadium to feel the Astroturf under his bare toes and got shut in overnight when the guards locked the gates.

A minute of silence follows the story's end. I break it, speak directly to the old builder. "I'm April," I say, "I talked to you on the phone, about volunteering, and you said you could use my help if I could stay for at least a week . . ."

"I know you's April," the old man grumbles, his voice sandpapery from cigarettes. "And you know I'm Don." He points at the other two in turn. "Them's Roger and Herbie. It's Herbie's house we're building." Herbie smiles at me, and I smile back. I try to guess his age—on the verge of high school? I'm relieved we've got a kid on the worksite to break up the tension that can build between adults with little in common, pleased to think this teen will get a home by the lake.

More silence. I squat down low to join them. We all watch Don examine his pear, then bite the brown star off the bottom and spit it five feet into the brush. He eats the fruit down to the skinny core, turns it sideways and eats the core in two bites, seeds and all. The stem he tosses, then wipes his hands on stained khakis and stands. We three rise after him and wait for his word.

"Well, boys, I think we'll get back to building," he says.

I'm the only non-boy on the site, and I wonder if his direction applies to me. Wiry ropes of muscle dance along his long, tan arms. Grey hair juts out around the bottom of his white painter's hat, and stubble sugars his face. His khakis and white t-shirt are splotched with mortar. Reaching into his pants pocket, he pulls out a red Bic lighter, slides a cigarette out of his shirt pocket, clicks a flame to life, holds it to the tip. Squinting and taking a drag, he asks me, "You ever a Girl Scout?"

"Yes, a while ago. I guess more than 15 years ago. When I was ten, maybe eleven. But sure, I was. Did the camping thing and all." My hands are gesturing in small tumbling motions in front of my belly, and I feel like I could keep blabbering, spewing out words to fill the wordless space he's left me, but I stop myself. "So yes," I whisper.

"Then you know how to build a fire." He tosses me the lighter, and I'm relieved to catch it. "See that pile of brush over there? You're gonna carry the brush to the sandpit and start it burning. Then you're gonna bring more to keep it burning. Probably take you the afternoon." He makes a "c'mon" motion to the boys with his dirty hand, and then they're striding toward the open cement slab to lay some more block. The little bit they've finished barely rises above the ground, looks like the crooked spine of a dinosaur they've unearthed.

I confront the mound of brush, as tall as the future house's imagined roof. I pledge to be sparing with my words for once, imagine dialogue that will mimic a John Wayne movie, with lots of "yeps" and "nopes." "Sure thing," I say to his back and angle off toward my job.

For fifteen minutes I hunch over the brush pile, ripping up bits of cardboard I found in a trash heap, trying to set them aflame. I arrange a scrap beneath a stick teepee, light it, blow tentatively, then hold my breath as it burns a while and peters out. I imagine eyes on my back as I lean over what should be a blaze. I clutch my last scrap of cardboard, mutter supplications over the sticks. Then I hear his feet on the ground behind me.

"Need my lighter," he says. I turn. He is tall above me. His lips dangle an unlit cigarette. I drop the lighter into his open palm. His fingers remind me of my grandfather Deda's, fat as sausages, with tough skin and thick nails. More paws than hands.

"That big pile a stuff's never gonna catch." He flicks the lighter to life. "Gotta get yourself a little pile to start with, all the paper in the middle." Isn't that what I was doing? Crouching down, he pulls a waxy Hostess cherry pie wrapper from his pocket, crumples it beneath sticks with a magician's sleight of hand, and within half a minute, flames crackle through the kindling. He drags a thick branch across the fire; sparks jump from the center. "So, you was a Scout, huh?" His eyes sparkle. "I ask all the young ones that and they always say yes, but they can never make a fire." He says "fire" like all my relatives near Pittsburgh—"fahr"—which makes me feel both linked to him and alien. I think of Deda tending the weekly garbage fire at the corner of his yard, of his 80-year-old brother who died after his clothes caught fire on burn day, with no one around to help him. Don shakes his head, turns back to the house-to-be.

I drag and burn brush for nearly three hours. My bare legs and arms are nicked and dirty. My mouth tastes like I've eaten Elmer's glue. After I feed the last bit of wood, I sit on the sand pile nearby and watch the rising shield of heat waver the trees beyond. When their rides come for them, the other two leave without looking my way—Herbie in a rusty blue Pinto driven by a gray-haired woman, Roger on the back of a young woman's motorcycle, without a helmet on his head or any possessions. When I tell Don I think I'm done, he nods and says, "Tomorrow then."

"What time?"

"Nine should do it. Doesn't pay to show up early."

Across the lake is my parents' cabin, where I'll stay alone this week. That night I unload a suitcase from my hatchback and carry it up the stone path to an A-frame made as much of windows as cedar siding. Sitting on the deck, surrounded by oak, hemlock, and pine, I eat leftover grilled chicken and veggie shish kabob made last night by my boyfriend, part of a sendoff dinner with friends at his rowhouse in the city. I'll have to go to the grocery store tomorrow.

It is strange to be so alone after nine months with talkative third graders, evenings in a houseful of roommates who love to talk politics and music and books, weekends in the city sharing space with other bike-riders and runners along Rock Creek Parkway, in bars where it's shoulder to shoulder waiting to shout at the bartender for a beer. On the weekend, the lake will be busy with water skiers and jet skiers and fisher-men, flowing in from Pittsburgh and DC and Baltimore, but now, on a Monday, the water is still, the houses bordering this cove empty. People must work during the week to pay for their weekend homes. Birds and squirrels chatter behind the silence.

I try to decide whether to shower away the afternoon's dirt or take a dip in the lake. Across the road and down the gravel path at the docks, the sun will still be shining on the water. With no one to push me in one direction or the other, I sit in a wooden Adirondack chair made by my dad, head back, eyes closed. Solitude feels both sweet and dangerous. My fire failure gnaws at me, becomes a berating voice: *If you can't even light a goddamn fire, what good are you? What practical skills have you got? Like they say: those who can, do—those who can't, teach. And in the summer you're nothing but a loafer. You rent a room in a house with transients—that's making a life? In DC, everyone's in flux. Maybe the New Yorkers are right— it isn't even a real city. It's a place that produces nothing but red tape.*

My best friend from childhood is pregnant with her first child. I'm happy for her but ashamed to admit I don't want a child myself. Spending all day with 25 kids is enough. Maybe securing a stable partner is a prerequisite to baby lust? With a boyfriend heading off to grad school in California, I feel an itch to light out, too—maybe a round-the-world trip, where I am the National Geographic photographer I once dreamed of becoming. When I was little, I had an Instamatic with a four-flash cube that turned to a fresh bulb once one side flashed and burned, and ever since I've been addicted to the way photos freeze and distill life. I was a yearbook photographer in junior and senior high. Photo albums line my shelves. And if I could travel the world now, I'd take the 35mm Nikon I got for high school graduation and explore the ways people have rooted themselves differently in different places: round mud huts in Southern Africa, white villas perched atop each other on the Greek Islands, red-tiled roofs in Mexico. Maybe even stone farmhouses in Croatia, my great-grandmother's homeland.

But these are my romantic visions of how people live. Maybe the way real people live is more like the sagging company houses along Main Street in my grandparents' coal town—not at all photogenic or picturesque. My great-grandmother Marija never had a house of her own until my grandfather and his brothers ordered a Sears kit and built one for her whole family late in her life. Before that, she took boarders into a company house, single miners who would provide income after her husband died and left her to raise nine kids alone.

Even if I did spend a summer traveling the world, snapping pictures of houses, I don't imagine it would count as doing something with my life. It's play, not work. Consumption, not production. And it requires not just time, which I have, but some serious money, which I don't.

One morning earlier this summer, soon after school let out, I sat with my coffee, reading the *Post*. My eyes drifted to my horoscope: "CAPRICORN: Don't hem and haw; take aim, and don't take no for an answer. If there is something you really want, do whatever it takes to follow through and make it happen. Being industrious will impress someone who can offer support." I am a believer in the power of horoscopes, not as predictors of the future, but as motivators. What did I really want to make happen? I stared out the window, willing it to appear before my eyes. How would the next few months be industrious? Other than a beach trip, a little curriculum development, and the basics of keeping one tiny life running, what would the summer days hold?

I dug through the pile of papers on my desk until I found the newspaper ad from the *Garrett County Gazette* I'd saved from a spring weekend at the lake. "Habitat for Humanity seeks volunteers—call Don." I left a message on his machine; he left a message on mine, with clipped instructions: "I'm out working on houses during the day. Call in the evening, not after 10, if you really want to do this."

"If?" Did he hear something in my recorded voice? Did I sound half-hearted? Most likely. I was half-hearted. Half of me wanted to pitch in, give back, contribute, justify my existence, work as hard as my parents and their parents and theirs before them had to work to deliver me to this moment. Half of me wanted selfish indulgence—to sleep late, lounge around the pool, read, cook intricate dinners with long lists of ingredients for friends.

One evening, between dinner and a show at the Source Theater with friends, I stepped into a phone booth on the corner of 14th and T Streets and pushed closed the hinged door, muffling the street sounds outside and triggering the light above. My jeans pocket drooped with quarters, and I pulled them out and placed them on the smooth stainless steel shelf beneath the phone. I picked one up and flicked it into the air with my thumb, caught it, and slapped it atop my other hand. I held it there momentarily, sweaty palm clinging to hand. "Heads, I go," I whispered, then lifted the hand like the top of a gift box. "Heads. Best two of three." All came up heads. The air in the booth grew stuffy. From my back pocket I pulled a slip of yellow paper, blue ballpoint scrawling his phone number. The quarter clanked its way through the phone, and I pressed the square metal keys to make the call.

Five long rings and then Don's gruff voice, "Yello?" I explained myself. "I can't guarantee I'll have work for you," he said. "Depends how far I get, what stage we're at. You can come or not come."

I saw myself alone in my parents' cabin for a week, potentially useless to this man. No TV to distract me. No friends. No theater. The blankness could engulf me, pull me under. But what would the days here hold, with all of my friends off working on the Hill or in government offices during the day and the sun beating down?

"Put me down for that week in July," I said. "At least a week. Write me down in pen. I'll be there."

"Suit yourself." (Did he really use that phrase, or did I ascribe it to him later?)

I heard a television in the background, a dog barking. I tried to imagine the builder watching TV shows pulled in by a big satellite dish on a desolate, wooded road. Was it news or sports or something else? I had slipped out at the intermission of a play called "Voices," which consisted entirely of five women delivering poetic monologues about their lives. I didn't know this man but already I imagined it wasn't something he'd go in for.

"Well, then," I said. "See you in July."

Twelve skinny miles long, Deep Creek Lake discharges into the Youghiogheny River (or the "Yock" to locals). The lake is a river really, dammed since 1925 for electric power. My mother came here as a girl in the 1950s, drove the hour and half south from Fairchance with her friend's family. My grandparents would never have been able to afford a trailer on the lake, let alone a boat, but the friend's father was a business-man, not a coal miner like many other men in town. Now that tiny lot on the lake is worth nearly a million.

The morning after the Girl Scout fire fiasco, I drive in the direction opposite the friends' place, where they've replaced the original trailer with a double-wide. If I could drive across the lakebed, I'd make it to the Habitat site in less than five minutes. The lake's curvy shore undulates for 65 miles, and the road along it bends around most of its water fingers, so it takes almost 30 minutes to drive the 10 miles to the site. Where the road comes close to the lake, I can see the mist resting on the water, a down comforter hovering. The sun has barely made it above the mountains, even by 8:30, and it feels weak, not enough rays yet to burn up the night's chill, so I am wearing a sweatshirt over my work clothes, gray with a black raven across the chest, our elementary school mascot. I try searching for a radio station, push all of my pre-set buttons automatically before I register that I'm not at home. I'm glad to forego the traffic reports, the reports of violence in city neighborhoods near my own. I turn the dial searching for morning news, but all I can find is country music and static, so I shut it off and drive in silence.

I am the only one on the site with Don for the first half hour, and I sip coffee from my plastic travel mug and wait as he putters around, pulling tools from the back of his battered silver Caravan, lining them up in a row on the rocky ground. I offer to help once. "Got my system," he says. I know not to offer again.

When Don is done, he looks up the slope at our cars. "Where the hell's that boy?" As if on cue, a muffler crescendos, and the Pinto pulls around the curve and comes to a stop. A glare on the glass obscures the driver, but when she leans forward, I see a halo of gray hair and her hand press against the windshield, in greeting or surrender. Herbie gets out slowly and takes mincing steps toward us. I wonder if he's hurt something—an ankle, perhaps—but his steps get stronger as he nears us, and I remember how difficult it was for my parents to get me up early when I was a teenager.

"Hey, Herbie," I say.

"No time to waste," says Don.

Herbie says nothing. His hair pokes up on top, like he's just rolled out of bed, and he picks at the inside corner of his right eye. I'm sure he didn't find time to eat breakfast, and I wonder what I might bring tomorrow that I could slip him—a granola bar, fruit roll-ups, a muffin? Would he eat a banana?

My first job today is building scaffolds with Herbie, connecting steel pipes into fittings, then laying boards over them to make a platform. The cinder block wall has reached high enough on the backside of the house to need the scaffold's height. The front, higher up the slope, hasn't even met ground level yet.

Once he's woken up, Herbie can't stop talking, telling me how excited his family is to be getting this house. "Yeah, my mom and sister can't stop with the plans. What kind of flowers they want to plant next summer.—*Ooh, what kind of curtains should we have for the picture window?*" He mimics them, but I can see his pride at serving as the family member who will put in the required 300 hours of "sweat equity" to qualify them for a Habitat house. "Yeah, I'm doin' my part now . . . they can do theirs later." Little man of the family dressed in a Transformers t-shirt too young for him and too tight for his fat belly.

I smile. "They're lucky to have you, Herbie."

We move on to mixing mortar. Herbie has done this earlier in the week, so he's the expert. "We need lots of sand. Shitloads. Hauling them buckets is a pain in the ass." He says this under his breath to me, conspiratorially. I'm not sure if it's the cuss words or the complaining he doesn't want Don to hear. I'm helping Herbie shovel sand from near the brush-burning site into white plastic buckets when the Pinto pulls up again. The grey-haired woman steps out and waves. "Don't mind me," she shouts, "I'm just here to watch my house bein' born."

"My mama," Herbie says, shaking his head like he wants to deny the connection. I wonder how she could be his mother, with her gray beauty shop hair and sagging body. She looks at least 55, but I'm shaky on ages much beyond my own 25 years. She's wearing a pink sleeveless housedress with pearly buttons down the front, flat red canvas shoes with a strap across the top. The smooth bottoms slip on the leafy bank as she approaches. The skin on her arms is slack, white, and papery—flesh jiggles like a rooster wattle as she holds her arms out for balance—while the skin on her legs is taught and shiny, muscles straining beneath the varicose veins and splotchy freckles.

"How you'uns holdin' up in the heat?" she asks, fanning her face dramatically with her hand. "It's a hot one."

The sun burns almost directly overhead, broiling the clearing. The shady woods encircle us and stifle any breeze that might make its way off the lake. But it's not humid hot like back in DC, only sunshiny hot, and it doesn't bother me. Up on the scaffold, Don grunts and keeps his face to the block wall. Herbie says, "I *am* hot. Did you bring me my Sprite?"

"Got it right here. Nice 'n cold, right out the icebox." She holds up the plastic bottle and when the sun hits it, it lights up like an electric emerald. Herbie uncaps it and chugs. All of a sudden I am thirsty. I grab my bottle of now-lukewarm water from beneath the bush where I stowed my stuff.

She looks at me and smiles, revealing gray teeth, and I introduce myself.

"Glad to meet you," she says, nodding, "Sure am happy to know there's another pair of hands around here."

Looking back at Herbie, who sits on the sand pile drinking his Sprite, she talks quickly, as if to fill in for Herbie's past and future lapses. "Can you believe I live in a trailer with a hole in the wall? I could see straight to the outside after Herbie's father kicked it clean through, but I patched it with some plywood. Rain still leaks through. Electric's spotty. Nobody's meant to live like that. Are they?"

I think of my mom's cousin, whose husband left her with two kids in a trailer plunked down behind her parents' bungalow. She couldn't find any work and finally gave up trying, relied on WIC and her mom and dad. Her father built a makeshift covered boardwalk between their two houses so that they could pass back and forth without snow or rain pelting them. Once when her toilet stopped working, she filled it with kitty litter until she could figure out where to get the money to fix it. Is that worse than a hole in a trailer wall? She's the one who stocked my grandparents' fridge with groceries when my Deda was recovering from his stroke. She waved away offers for repayment. One day she would deliver homemade Italian Wedding Soup, with tiny meatballs formed by hand, and the next it would be a lasagna. How are we meant to live? The best way we know how.

I shake my head, wondering where Herbie's father is now. "Let's hope these walls hold up better than that," I say. Using the long-handled hoe, I mix the mortar in a huge, banged-up steel mortar pan. The wet mortar seems heavier than the components combined. When I pull it toward me hard, it feels like rowing a heavy johnboat.

"More goop," yells Don, and I switch to the shovel and plop a bunch in the bucket Don has handed down to me from up on the scaffold. Now I'm starting to sweat, and I wish I'd worn a bandana or a baseball cap as I wipe my hairline with the bottom edge of my T-shirt.

"You are one skinny Minnie," the mother declares, staring at my stomach. "I remember when I had a waistline. You don't have no kids?" I shake my head. My mother had two babies by the time she was 25. Herbie's mom goes on chatting about her plans for the house, how she'll sit at the picture window in the winter with her cup of coffee and look out through the bare trees to the lake. Seems she doesn't know or recall that Pennelec drains the lake in the winter and this cove will just be a cracked muddy bottom, but I don't want to ruin her dream, so I say nothing. She keeps looking back at Herbie, who has lain back now with his forearm over his eyes.

"Oh, my," she says. She talks loud enough for Don to hear. "Herbie woke up with one of his migraines again this morning. They lay him out, boy. We are fresh out of his meds, and wouldn't you know the doctor's not in today. I'm not sure he's gonna last." She looks nervously up at Don, who does not respond. I can sense him bristling.

"April, gonna need more block up here shortly."

"Yep," I say and start toting. I take two cinder blocks from the stack and set them tallwise on the ground before slipping my hands into the open squares. Carrying them the 20 yards and lifting them up to Don strains my fingers, but the pull at my elbow and shoulder joints is pleasing, the equal weight evening me out. The rough edges scrape at the sides of my knees every few steps, so I'm glad I wore jeans today.

Herbie's mom hovers over him, then comes back to us, struggling to carry a block on her way. I take it from her when she sets it down for the third time. "Damn it all, he's throwing up," she says to me. "We're between a rock and a hard place, we are." She pulls a white handker-chief embroidered with yellow roses from her pocket and wipes at her nose. I wouldn't believe anyone living in the late 20th century would still use hankies, but I've seen my grandmother slip one from inside her sleeve while shopping at Kmart or just doing housework. "Damn it," she whispers, then turns her voice up to Don and yells, "I'll have him back tomorrow once I get that there doctor on the phone. You can bet on it."

I watch Herbie shuffle to the car with his mom's arm around him, and I feel sorry for this young boy on whose shoulders this house rides. Don snorts as they pull away. He mutters, "Good riddance." He sees my face and adds, "This ain't the first time. It's an all-the-time thing, April." He pulls a spiral notebook and golf pencil out of his pocket and makes a few scribbles.

"You writing him a ticket?" I ask.

"I have to keep track of the hours. It's a requirement. Three today. Hardly enough."

A timesheet for a thirteen-year-old. No one makes me account for my time, but sometimes I do it anyway—track the way I've spent my hours with a reckoning in my journal. Cleaned the kitchen floor (for roommates who don't care if I do or don't). Chopped vegetables at the soup kitchen for two hours. Read one chapter in a book on autism. Unlike Don's notebook, my tally sheet means nothing to anyone but me, has no bearing on what I earn or where I live.

It's just me and Don at the worksite now, and it feels a little funny to be sitting on the hillside eating where he and the other guys sat yesterday. The scene of Don throwing me the lighter feels like a month ago. I ask about the guy from yesterday, Roger, and he tells me why Roger was here in the first place: arrested for DWI, unemployed, couldn't pay the fine, so the judge gave him community service.

"He's not comin' back, I'll tell you that right now. All of them look-ing to pay their debt to society with nothing but themselves. Looking for some credit with their sorry asses as collateral. Can't even pay what they owe that way, let alone get ahead." There's a bitterness in his chuckle. I want to say, *"Herbie's only a boy,"* but before I can, he asks, "How about you, April? Who do you owe?" I don't know whether it's a friendly ques-tion or a trick.

"I'm free and easy," I say, "no debts, no strings." But I could tell him lots of people I owe, if I thought he really wanted to hear it. I'd start with my great-grandmother Marija. What did she envision when she lit out for life in a new country, landing alone in New York? Did she envision the nine children she bore in just over a decade? She certainly could not have envisioned her husband dead from the Spanish Flu, leaving her alone to raise the kids, or the way his death meant that my grandfather, her eldest son, had to drop out of school in the sixth grade to work in the mines.

"No debts," Don says, "And yet you're here." His cigarette butt sizzles as he drops it into his Coke can.

"I'm here."

"And neither of those other debtors are. So, it's you and me to pick up their slack."

That day, we lay three more rows of block on the basement walls, and Don calls it a good day. We're cleaning up, washing the trowel and mortar pan out, and I'm looking at my hands and how torn up and chapped they've gotten, thinking whether I saw any lotion back at my parents' place. I wonder whether it's possible to rub off your fingerprints. It seems like the ridges on my right pointer finger are gone. "You need yourself some gloves," Don says.

"Yeah, I was thinking to stop by Naylor's Hardware on the way home. Need anything?"

"I got extras. I'll bring you some. Your reward for working hard." He's holding a slender, smooth steel rod in his hand, tapping it against his palm, then he lifts it out toward me like something holy, like the priest offering communion. "See this? Know what it is?"

"I know you've been using it between the blocks."

"Called a striking tool. Finishes off the mortar joints. Tomorrow I'm promoting you to striker." He bows his head slightly and raises his eyebrows, leaning in close and staring at me to see if I understand the import of this move.

"Good. I'm ready for a change."

On Day Three, it's just me and Don again all morning long, building the walls. He starts by showing me how to make a smooth line along the mortar joint after he muds and lays the block. He doesn't have to tell me how a missed line will dry if I wait too long to strike it. I am on it. The sound of steel on sand on cinder block is gritty, soothing and rhythmic all at once, and we work together in this sound and the absence of words until we hear the car door above us. Here comes Herbie down the slope with a paper bag in his hand, and I realize I'm hungry and it will be time for lunch soon. Don sighs. His trowel lands in the bucket with a clank.

The mom offers no explanation for their tardiness. "Turns out he's got to *eat* more often. Doctor says the headaches can be triggered by hunger." Herbie stands a foot behind her nervously rolling and fraying the top of the brown paper bag. He's already got that belly that hangs over the waistband, so I doubt that he doesn't eat often enough. Or maybe he doesn't eat the right things. The way he moves—haltingly, clumsily—makes me doubtful he plays sports, but does he have a bike to ride?

"Hey, Herbie," I say. "Feeling better?" He nods his head, but keeps his eyes down.

Don looks at his watch. "May as well eat now. You hungry now, Herbie?" He tries his best to say it kindly, but I can hear an undercurrent.

Herbie shrugs. "Can always eat."

The mom looks at each of us in turn, relieved that people are talking. "Well, I'm glad we're all set. Got to get back to Sissy," she says to Herbie. Today she has on yellow stretch pants, and as she struggles and puffs up the slope, the elastic waistband pulls down to reveal the top of her sheer white undies.

After lunch, Don assigns Herbie to mixing mortar and carrying block. Each time Herbie returns with a block, he stays a minute to watch me. After a few trips, he asks, "Can I do that? How about we trade jobs for a while?" Don is off somewhere. I'm alone with Herbie. A hardness rises up in me unexpectedly, like I've drunk the mortar and it's just now set. I try to stop myself, but words slide out in a tight, prim voice, "Well, you'll have to ask Don," knowing Don won't let him. "It's not as easy as it looks. It took me the whole morning to get it right." As if I'm an expert. As if it's not just sliding a steel bar along a wet line. I am queasy listening to myself defend what feels like my territory, the way I offer these lame excuses to a boy.

Later that afternoon, Herbie is dragging a bucket of sand, walking backwards in rhythmic steps, doing his best Michael Jackson slide, singing "Billy Jean is not my lover," when his heel bumps up against the mortar pan and he falls backward into it. It's like a cartoon, that expression on his face, his mouth a big O. His arms and legs sprawl out in an X, his bottom sunk in the muck. He's frozen there for a minute, until Don lets out a hoot of laughter. "Damn, Herbie, you're up a crick now. That stuff dries damn fast." This is the most animated I've seen Don. His eyes dance. I know he doesn't view this as his problem.

Leaning over and extending my hand, I pull Herbie up until he stands in front of me stiffly. "Let's get you to the lake," I say. I use some newspaper to slough off as much of the mortar from his backside as I can. With the seat folded down in the back of my hatchback, he just fits lying on his stomach with his feet up in the air. Each bump in the road puffs an "oof" from his mouth, but he doesn't say anything. I drive to the state park beach and tell him to go for a swim. It's not crowded on a weekday, but a few families with small children play in the sand and watch him curiously as he trudges to the edge of the water farthest from them, takes off his Nike running shoes, and wades in. He floats on his back and waves to me as I sit on the hood to wait. "Watch this, April," he shouts, then does a handstand in the water and flips over backward, and I laugh loud enough for him to hear.

When he comes out dripping, most of the mortar has washed away, but enough residue remains along the seams of his jeans that I know we'll have to mention it to his mom. "Good as new," I say, swiping at a gray clump clinging to his back pocket.

He's not worth much for the rest of the day, and the next day we don't see him. Don doesn't say anything about it, so I stay silent on the matter, too. Instead I ask a few questions about Don's life, and I'm surprised when pieces of his story tumble out one after the other. How he was a builder all of his adult life and retired five years ago. How his wife died two years back of lung cancer. How he dropped out of school after ninth grade. He looks at me shyly when he tells me that. "You must think that's awful, you bein' a teacher and all."

"Those were different times," I say.

"I'm taking an English class now, over at the community college," he offers.

"Wow, I'm impressed," I say, but what I really am is curious about what makes someone depart so radically from his life's trajectory in his 70s. What he hopes to gain.

He must see my doubt. "Maybe I'll write the next Moby Dick." He chuckles. "Or at least a good fish story."

On Day Five, my final day, Herbie is AWOL again, and toward the end of the day Don comes and stands next to me while I'm striking. He doesn't do anything, just stands, so I stop and look at him. "Talked to the project coordinator on the phone last night. Thought I should let you know we're gonna have to remove the house from Herbie's family." I imagine a huge truck towing this foundation away. Don sees I'm perplexed. "It's a damn shame, April, but there's lots of people waiting for a house, and the program's got rules. A big part of it is them working for themselves, proving themselves."

"Can't my hours this week count toward their sweat equity?" I argue.

"Don't work that way. Can't work that way. You and I can't pull 'em up. Besides, they'd still be short."

"Who are we building this house for now?"

"There's a list. The office'll find a new family.

"What will happen to Herbie's family?" I am full of questions, most of which he can answer, but I know he can't answer that one. He and I are both silent for a while. "Will you tell him I'm sorry?"

He looks at me sharply. "You got nothing to be sorry for."

"Yeah. Maybe," I say softly.

He shifts the conversation. "I know you was supposed to go back tonight. Maybe you'd consider one more day. Walls'll be done by midday if you'd stay." So I stay.

That evening, my last night on the lake, I walk down the gravel path as I've done after each day's work. Days in the trees leave me anxious for open views. Something in my chest feels like a skittering animal in a cage, until I see the gleam of water in slats through the trees, and I breathe out in long relief. I take in the stretch of late sun laid out like a golden platter for me, take it in through eyes and skin and nose, and then I move toward the water.

At the end of the communal dock, I climb to the back of my dad's motorboat, stand on the top rung of its ladder. I know myself well enough to know that if I feel the water, its chill will prevent me from diving, so I do not dip my toe in, just dive flat out like a racer, smack the water's surface with my torso and swim freestyle fast until my body pushes the cold away. As I approach the other side of the cove, I ease into breaststroke. My movements ripple the water, otherwise glassy at this end of the lake. Some days, near the grasses on the bank, I've met with a wood duck, whose squawk so close always startles me. Its iridescent green head, orange eyes, and beak seem too colorful for the tan grasses and murky lake water.

A string of days away from home—even a short one—can form a rhythm so quickly, start to feel like your whole existence, like this is how your life is and will be. Days of staring at block after block, pan after pan of mortar, have been a way to clear my mind of the past, of questions about what I should be doing. It has been simply "move the block, strike the mortar line, clean the tools," all of this right here before you now.

But on this last night here on the lake, I see that the days of building have not cleared my mind, just packed the junk away for storage. I see that it will never be cleared. When I take in the long blank view of the lake, ribbons of thought unwind across the water. My mind turns to Herbie, what causes his migraines and how they will be cured, where his family will end up living, whether they would have been able to keep up the house if they had gotten it.

I rub my forehead and shield my eyes from the glare. Then in the glint of sun on water my great-grandmother Marija visits me, and I see her shaking her head— judging or marveling, I can't be sure. I wonder what she would think of this great-granddaughter swimming through life unencumbered by husband, children, home. That I have squandered her suffering? *A lady of leisure,* I hear her say. But then I feel her finger tracing my palm in tiny circles, as she did when I was a child living in the house my grandfather built her. I sit on her lap and she sings a song in Croation as she holds my hand. *Mali mišji,* she intones, her voice high, her face close to mine. "Mouse, mouse, where have you gone? Not in the barn? Look, on the wall!" And then I have to look away as she puts a coin in my hand. *I see you have made it out, little mouse. Good for you.*

The next morning, Saturday, I take my camera to the work site. The weekenders are here, and even early, the lake is buzzing with motorboats trailing water skiers. I snap a few photos of the lake glistening through the trees. But when Don suggests he take my picture by the back wall of the house, I find I do not want him looking at me through the lens of my camera, do not want him to frame me, pin me in a tiny rectangle of the negative. Even in the print, the cinder block wall will seem thin and light, and I will seem big and eager next to it. I do not want to see what I look like here, how little I've really done. I think to say, "let me take your picture and I'll send it to you," something very like me, but I don't say it. I take one image of the walls, then put the lens cap on and snap the cover closed. "That all?" Don asks.

"That's all," I say, then shake his hand.

In the car, I fast forward to my boyfriend, who will ask later tonight to see the tan lines left by my T-shirt. *Farmer tan*, he will laugh. The back of my neck is a deep chestnut, a sharp contrast to the honey color of my back. He will see remnants of the work, but they are not the work. He might have liked to see a photo, but that is not the work. I hear Don's final words to me: "Thanks a million, you were a big help." The summer will wear on, the sun will burn down, the words will fade, the tan will fade. No matter how much mortar we mix, how much block we lay, it will never be enough.

NONFICTION

Pittsburgh's Annie Dillard declared, "The essay can do everything a poem can do and everything a short story can do—everything but fake it." This is true of all nonfiction. Each piece must hold the reader's attention through vivid imagery, clarity of voice, development of its idea, and (to fulfill the *Northern Appalachia Review's* mission) be grounded in regional geography, all without falsifying information. That "truth" is usually hard-won and not gained without extraction and reclamation—extraction from a physical place or from one's sense of self, reclamation as a reckoning with and ultimate acceptance of the past before reassembling a new landscape. This reckoning manifests into many poignant confessions, containing elements of nostalgia, shame, curiosity, and determination, among others. Grounded in truth, the significance of its strata can only be viewed through intense observation and reflection.

While many of the submitted pieces capture the landscape of northern Appalachia, an overlooked aspect of our region, or a particular character's voice, the ones included in the inaugural issue resonate beyond place and person. The pieces chosen for this issue are not simply verbal portraits of the landscape or a singular character, but are layered personal histories which reveal this region is not limited to its extractive industrial past or its unique personas. Family histories, childhood haunts, hidden rules, and daily life have inspired the words within this section. Below the surface though, these accounts grapple with insecurities on body image, with loss and disconnection. They address escape, acceptance, and return; an environmental progression rooted in personal geography; and an unshakable determination.

Even as my criteria for selecting individual work for this section relied heavily on the ability of each piece to stand well as nonfiction, the overarching goal was to include pieces whose relationship to northern Appalachia was as varied and multi-layered as the strata of bedrock, sandstone, and shale seen while driving along the highways toward our homes.

—Carrie Hohmann Campbell, Nonfiction Editor

Northern Appalachia Review – Nonfiction

Of Outhouses and Humiliation

by Christina Fisanick

I take a deep breath and squat, my skin barely touching the seat of the outhouse toilet. I pee as fast as possible, wipe, and toss. I nearly break into a run fleeing the small, reeking confines of the camp latrine. You see, I have been in mortal fear of using outhouses since childhood.

It took me decades to figure out why I feared sitting my bare bum over a gaping hole in the Earth. The stench itself should be enough, but it wasn't just that. And it wasn't my horror-movie fear of a giant anaconda slurping up out of the muck and carrying me off to his fetid lair. As it turns out, my fear of outhouses is baked in—genetically woven into my corporeal code.

The story goes like this. My Great Aunt Creasy went to the family outhouse one summer day, broke the toilet seat and pedestal platform, and then crashed through the floor. She landed several feet below, "up to her neck in raw shit."

The storyteller's tone was always 90% serious and 10% humorous—whether it was my grandfather, mother, or one of Creasy's siblings. Although the teller sometimes changed how many hours it took to fish Great Aunt Creasy out ("She dog paddled in that shit until the next morning." "Brownie's Wrecker got there right after supper.") or what she said as she screamed and cried for help ("Lord, get me out!" "Davey Earl, get the block and tackle!"), two details remained the same throughout the tellings: Great Aunt Creasy wore fire engine red lipstick way beyond the boundaries of her lip lines, and "she was a big, big woman."

Now, clearly, a story like this would frighten most children who might have the need to visit an outside toilet, but for me it became a defining narrative about the bodies of women, my body, and fat.

As my battle with binge eating disorder worsened, my weight increased and I internalized messages about body hate and fat. Great Aunt Creasy's plight exemplified for me the reality of being a fat woman, and only years later did I realize that my fear of outhouses wasn't about pissing in a dark hole in the ground, but about the shame I would face if I broke the toilet seat and fell into the filth below.

Subconsciously for years and then consciously for many more, I wondered about the increasingly fewer cases I needed to use an outhouse, if my weight now was enough to break the seat. Had I become "a big, big woman"? Would this be the time my too-heavy body finally pulled the trigger and made me the subject of generations of family lore?

On the surface, it is a good story, right? It's not every day that some-one has to be hauled out of a latrine by a tow truck. But I wonder now as I wondered then if my family was trying to entertain me and my cousins or warn us all by repeating Great Aunt Creasy's potentially fatal accident. After all, this is the ONLY story I've ever heard about her. It's all I know of a woman—my own flesh and blood—and her time on this Earth.

In my marrow, I feared such a legacy while still deep in the throes of binge eating disorder. I had internalized Great Aunt Creasy's humiliation. Her shame had become my shame. I became her—a woman kicking and thrashing to stay afloat in a pond of shit her family had created. This fear and shame eventually extended to other areas of my life as I found myself carefully testing porch swings to see if they could hold my weight; easing gently into my own bathtub, pausing with a racing heart at the slightest creak; and generally holding my breath in life, not just because I didn't want my bathtub to come crashing through the ceiling, but because of a generations-deep fear of the shame I'd feel because everyone would know that it wasn't a rotted floorboard that caused the crash, but the weight of "a big, big woman."

Behind Closed Doors

by Kip Knott

Back in 1973, a quarter painted fire-cracker red was worth more to me and my siblings than all the money in the world. Not just any quarter painted fire-cracker red would do, though. The red quarter that we coveted came from the cash register of the Stonefront Tavern, a dimly lit and perpetually dusty bar in the heart of Ohio coal country. With that red quarter, as well as some unexplained magic, any one of us could walk over to the darkest corner of the Stonefront and conjure our favorite song from the gleaming chrome and neon Zenith jukebox. Whether it was actually true or whether it is my memory being filtered through the cloud of nostalgia that hangs in my mind the way cigarette smoke hung in the bar, I can't say; however, I remember that jukebox being mostly populated with single-after-single of the greatest Country & Western songs of the day, and some long before the day. Despite the slim pickings of pop and rock songs on the jukebox, my brother Kevin, the oldest of us at 17, looked for any song that wasn't a C & W staple, usually settling on Neil Young's "Heart of Gold." My sister Kim, just a year younger than Kevin, always chose anything by Willie Nelson because she loved the way that I, with my pre-pubescent 11-year-old voice, could perfectly imitate his signature nasal twang. For middle-child Kelly, Neil Diamond was her man and "Holly Holy" was her song. At only seven years old, Patrick, the youngest, loved "Candy Man" by Sammy Davis, Jr., possibly the only song by a black singer in the entire jukebox. Whenever it was my turn to choose, though, I always made what I thought was the most chivalrous choice, Charlie Rich's "Behind Closed Doors," because it was the bartender's favorite song. The moment those first tinny piano notes would break through the din of PBR bottles clinking on Formica tables and the pop of shot-glasses banged down on the battered oak bar, the 60-year-old woman with bright red hair and horn-rimmed glasses behind the bar would smile and cackle her approval. "Thank you," my grandmother would yell to me over the husky mumble of smoky voices, before turning to pour a shot of Jack for a gray-faced miner trying to dull the pain of his aching body at the end of his shift.

The Stonefront was a very special place for me and my siblings, and we spent many happy hours of our childhood in its smoke-and-profanity-filled environment because that was where our grandmother worked for ten years after she retired. The bar was nestled next to Sunday Creek—a tiny, sulfurous tributary of Burr Oak Lake that slithered through Perry County, Ohio, like a sickly orange snake—in the little coal-mining town of Corning. My grandparents, Tod and Margaret Knott, were both born in Hemlock, a small village outside of Corning, in 1913 and 1914 respectively. Both were raised in Perry County, so when they retired—he from Ohio State and she from a shoe factory in Columbus—they moved to a house just outside of town that my grandfather had built with his own two hands on weekends over a period of twelve years. Both of my grandparents were workaholics, so retirement for them was an opportunity to move on to something new: for my grandfather, that meant grave digging; for my grandmother, that meant tending bar.

When Grandma first started tending bar at the Stonefront in 1970, the miners didn't quite know how to react. Even though Gwen, the wife of the bar's owner, frequented the bar every night, she herself never tended the bar, opting instead to sit on a specially padded barstool at the far end of the bar away from the door, her miniature white poodle Cindy asleep in a cardboard beer box lined with multi-colored yarn blankets my grandmother had crocheted especially for her. At first, the miners treated Grandma with a cold distance that I'm sure they thought equaled respect, calling her Mrs. Knott whenever they asked for a drink. When one of the miners inevitably tried to push the bounds of decency to see if Grandma would crumble, she shot back, "Look here. You can't shit a shitter. I carry a turd in each pocket." From that moment on, my grandmother went from being known as Mrs. Knott to being called "Babe," the nickname that my grandfather had always called her. And from that moment on, Babe became the favorite bartender to the coal-caked miners who stumbled through the battered wooden door with the diamond window for a beer or a shot of whatever medicine soothed their tired bodies.

At least six times a year my family would pack up the green behemoth Oldsmobile Vista Cruiser station wagon—a vehicle that was more boat than car and that easily accommodated all seven of us as well as our dog, Max—and travel four-and-a-half hours from Farmington Hills, Michigan, to Perry County. Inevitably, our first stop after unpacking the car would be the Stonefront to see Grandma. My brothers and sisters and I would go through the motions of saying hello to Grandma, but it was the red quarter that we really wanted to see. Before we could even ask her to pluck it from the large brass National cash register perched on a shelf against the long mirror that ran the length of the wall behind the bar, Grandma would enlist us to wash greasy glasses, empty the trash that smelled of cigarette butts and stale peanuts, and sweep the linoleum floor stained a permanent gray by decades of dirty miners' boots.

"Why don't you just give 'em the quarter, Babe," piped up Kermit Sarvis, a Stonefront regular as well as Grandma's cousin. (Truth be told, nearly every other person who came through the doors of the Stonefront populated some branch of our extensive family tree.)

"You go on and let them finish their jobs," Grandma shot back. "They know the rules."

Once all of our chores were completed, Grandma would inspect our work, click her dentures as she assessed the quality of our completed tasks, and invariably say, "Good work," before cranking the cash register open and handing the red quarter over to Kevin, who always got first pick. Together we'd hustle over to the jukebox as a collective mass, watch Kevin drop the quarter down the slot, and almost cheer as we listened to it clatter through the metallic innards of the machine before it reappeared in the change slot at the bottom. The reappearance of the coin was the most magical part of the entire process, because for children who had been raised Catholic, it was akin to the miracle of Jesus rising from the dead after three days: the red quarter had traveled through the shadow of the valley of death only to return to us so that we could send it forth once again to resurrect our ability to choose one more song.

It didn't take long before my siblings and I became like surrogate children to the miners, and we never wanted for anything while we were there. Whereas my grandmother would never give us anything free, the miners were always sneaking us two-bits so we could buy a spicy pickled sausage that reeked of vinegar and brine or a bottle of Orange Crush that filled our mouths with sweet citrus syrup and stained our tongues traffic cone orange. The bone-weary men especially loved it when we sang along with the songs we'd chosen on the jukebox, yelling out requests for some of their own favorites: "Do the one about the sunshine and the shoulders!"; "How 'bout some Hank Williams?"; "Play 'Cool Water' by Sons of the Pioneers!" And we'd oblige them every time, knowing that we'd receive some treat in exchange, but not knowing that what we were giving to them was something far more valuable: a moment of happiness and light after hours spent in the dark with the weight of the world bearing down on them.

When Grandma finally fully retired in 1980, she—and, by extension, we kids—left the bar behind for good. She and Grandpa lived a quiet life in the house he had built with his own two hands until his death in 1998. Unable to keep the house up to her exacting standards alone, Grandma sold the house and moved from Perry County to a retirement home in Columbus, where she lived until her death in 2004. During those years, my brothers and sisters and I all went off to college, got jobs, had kids, and found new bars to frequent, new bartenders to cozy up to, and new jukeboxes to play.

A few years ago, my sister Kim drove down to Corning with her son Christian, now a grown man of 30. Kim wanted to show Christian the Stonefront so he could see for himself the place that held some of her fondest memories.

"Corning," she told me, "is virtually a ghost town, with most of the buildings on Main Street vacant and boarded up." Like so many towns in Perry County, Corning had become a casualty of the depressed coal mining industry.

"The building next to the Stonefront is completely gone," she continued. "The Stonefront itself is still there, but it looks like it's been closed for a long time. The front door is boarded up and padlocked. When we looked through the window on the door, we could see the big Stonefront Tavern sign sitting in the middle of the floor. All the tables are gone. Christian thought that we should try to find a way to buy the sign to give to Dad."

"That's a great idea," I told her. "Let's do it!"

"We already tried," she replied forlornly. "When we got back, we did some research and found a number online to call about renting buildings in Corning. I called it, but the number had been disconnected."

Disconnected. I realized at that moment how disconnected I had become from the Stonefront. Over the years I had disconnected myself from it and the miners who had shown me and my siblings nothing but kindness and gratitude. I thought a long time about that sign sitting in the middle of the bar. I promised myself that I would look into ways of trying to purchase the sign and bring it back into the light. But the realities of life soon took precedence, and one day would pass without me doing anything, then another, then a month, and then . . . and then . . . As far as I know, the sign remains behind closed doors like a memory that is too painful and too sweet to remember.

Spontaneously Aborted

by Rondalyn Whitney

Route 60 winds, curvaceous, past farms, the public pool, and Kawana Vista Park, where all the 4-H'ers, girl scouts and boy scouts met on picnic tables, sheltered by shingled awnings. I learned early how to take the curves—ease off of the gas when you enter, accelerate as you exit the curve. About a mile up on that road is my mother's house, right at the crossroads. My dad built that house himself, placed the two-by-fours 12 inches apart instead of the 18 inches required by building codes. We moved into that 3-bedroom brick house on my 5th birthday. My bedroom windows faced Route 60 as it stretched out into the only short straight path for miles, broken lines to signal you could, at last, pass.

My brother and I rode our bikes to the pool each day in the summer. Ed was the senior lifeguard, taught all of us how to swim across the pool, retrieve quarters off the bottom of the deep end, and perform a cannonball off the high dive.

We played baseball in the backyard, the apple and peach trees were first and second, touching third meant rounding the boxwood. Home, always, was just a tramped down spot easy to find in the summer grass. I was good at sports until I grew into a 36C overnight, underwire bras heralding the sacrifice of a smooth swing that propelled the ball in a straight arc above and beyond the peaches. Neighbors often came to play. My brother's friends were like brothers themselves, sleeping on our floor, asking me to hem their jeans, begging me to make another baloney sandwich or seven. They were most admiring of my well-known Best 2-egg cake.

I remember the day I turned—it was an unspectacular fall afternoon and my brother, John Martin and I were playing two-hand touch in the yard. I managed, finally, to get my hands on John. That day, though, instead of a congratulations, he laughed, a chilling laugh—I had touched below the belt. Not a foul in football, but a crime of puberty. I never played with them again.

Drew and I, along with Kyle, got baptized at the Union Church, dunked full immersion in the pond, wearing clothes and shoes. The congregation sang "Amazing Grace" and "Gather at the River." Kyle was a drummer, said he heard drumbeats when he went under, but I only felt the warmth, even though it was January. Drew and Kyle were the first to come to the funeral home when my dad died the summer between junior high and high school. Heart attack took him at 41.

At lunch, I sat on the bench outside with my three best friends, Robin, Lisa and Mary. We weren't in the top tier of the popularity caste system but instead in our own tier—we genuinely liked farmer's kids from the ridge, the *Jocks*, and the *Brains*. We were Switzerland in the world of high school drama. Our mothers made our clothes. We read fashion magazines, where I learned that with straight hair, oils secreted from the scalp find an easy path traveling down the shaft to the end, hydrating along the way. With curls, the journey is longer and with too many turns so that the oils surrender. We ironed our curls, smashed them into the day's popular straightened style, defiantly resisting our genetic predisposition for frizz.

In high school, I had a job writing for the town newspaper. The paper was small and the editor, Mr. Dudley, managed to get enough ads from the local businesses to pay us a little. He wasn't a kind man, just reliably disinterested. I reviewed the newest albums and wrote a weekly feature column or opinion piece. I interviewed Dick Clark when he came to town. I won a national writing contest for two poems and was published in an anthology. But my mother refused to buy it; she didn't want to encourage such frivolity.

I was a good student, had the reputation as a "smart girl," president of the glee club, alto in the *acapella* choir. Had I been a boy, I would have studied physics and calculus in high school. Since I was a girl, that wasn't suggested. I finished dissecting the frog after Drew passed out, and together, we both aced the exam with 100%. I completed my last math class, geometry, with an A, earned my seat in Mu Alpha Theta Math Honor Society with Drew and Mark and fell in love with Topology and Transcendental numbers. I dated a football player, listened to Casey Kasem's top 100 each weekend on WKEE. I had a plan. I was going to college. I knew how to become a teacher or a nurse but secretly I was plotting to become a journalist. That seemed rebellious at the time. I broke up with my football player boyfriend when he got angry with me when I told him I had applied to college.

I suppose it's true to admit I was progressive, even then. Miss Brown sent me to the principal's office when, in typing class, she said I needed to work on reducing my errors "so the man I work for will not be displeased." I told her I wasn't planning to work for a man, but wanted to learn to type my term papers in college. *She* was displeased. The principal, Mr. Fitz, was amused when he read my pink slip. He bought me a diet Coke from the teacher's lounge. Later, he would come to my book signing at Barnes & Noble.

Cheri was a cheerleader, had one of those sparkly smiles and was voted to be in the homecoming court, ride on the float. But after she got pregnant, she was quietly exited off the cheerleader team. Her fashionably short haircut grew out and became a quickly twisted ponytail, and she started wearing oversized gray sweats to school. She sort of faded away as her body swelled bigger and bigger, and then she disappeared entirely right before the end of 10th grade. I don't know what became of her—she's not in any pictures in the yearbook. I didn't know then to wonder who the father of her child was, it was just the story of a girl, of shame, of one to look away from. Unwed, tarnished, soiled, she would have to bear a woodscolt, a bastard, a mistake. Her life was over.

Mary and I made a pact, then. If either of us got pregnant we would step out into traffic before the sin of sex was obvious. Neither of us had had sex then but we watched what happened to Cheri. She didn't have a shower like the young married girls would, and baby pictures were never passed—she just faded into the fabric of a town's hushed rumors.

By my senior year of high school, Ed, that lifeguard, died. By then I had learned he liked to hire high school girls to come to his house and baby sit for his children. None of us ever saw his children, they were tucked in bed and asleep when we arrived. Mary lost her virginity to one of those nights of sitting for him as did, I suspect, many of my other classmates. I wasn't sorry when I heard he had died, choking on his own vomit in his sleep. Even now when I think of him, I smell chlorine and rotted trash.

The summer of my senior year, Lisa married, then, 37 weeks later, had a son, the first of four, all before she turned 23. I went to college, studying English, until the chair of the department, a short man, grew overly fond of the legs on my 5'8" frame. He would stare at me while we were supposed to be editing for syntax and line length, and say *You know, young lady, it's better to have loved a short man than never to have loved a tall.* I suppose he found that witty; I found it invasive. This was so normal, back then. I changed my major to psychology. I went on to earn a master's degree in Occupational Therapy and a doctorate in *International Health Science.* I learned multilinear regression, how to statistically determine risk and protection factors in data related to HIV transmission, calculate type I and type II errors. I never took another class in the English department.

When I went to my 30th high school reunion, I won the prize for having the youngest child, my second son, born when I turned 44. George Turner handed me the prize—a box of condoms. Ha. Ha. My husband does not remember any of this. George is a favorite in our class, voted vice president back in the day, well liked. He never had children. I hear George is in the hospital getting a double lung transplant. I unfriended him on Facebook after he posted a series of rants against welfare moms and Obama, but sometimes he still posts a comment on my page. One of our mutual friends recently posted a request for "prayers for George." I do hope his lungs give him new breath, but I feel conflicted about my tax dollars and Obama's Affordable Care Act footing the bill for his lungs. I feel petty for thinking this way. I do not pray for him.

The child that won me the box of condoms was born while I was in my doctoral program. He was three when I finished my dissertation, and four when I earned my degree. Had I been a boy, I suppose, I would have gone to medical school with Drew (Dermatologist) and Mark

(Veterinarian). There are just three of us with the honorific of doctor, me the only girl.

These days, I have two boys and a husband, a dog, Aetna health insurance and a 401K. I am a clinical professor in the school of medicine, where I teach and conduct research. I am completing a secondary analysis of data related to adverse childhood experiences, demonstrating how early stress changes the mother at the level of her genetic code, which means she passes it along epigenetically to her offspring, born to flail.

Each summer I volunteer at a camp in rural Appalachia. The camp is for children with severe disabilities, and their families. I have pictures of me from my time at camp. I am holding a 2-year-old prone across my outstretched legs, his arms stretching down into a tub of bubbles. His small hands fish for the dinosaurs I have hidden in the soapy slurry. His oxygen tube is anchored securely below his nose then twists around his small head before it travels around my own leg and back to the pump. He was a micro-preemie, born too early, before his lungs were ready for air. His mother, sixteen at the time, says "he just fell out of me." This is the first time he has tolerated sticky sensations on his hands, or unexpected splashes on his face. I am grateful for my education and clinical experience. The mother is grateful her boy can play. I imagine the hospital when this child came—23 weeks, weighing just 1 pound. The team would have intubated and warmed and worked with dogged determination to save this one little spurt of a boy.

I lost 6 babies, miscarried at 4, 6, 6, 7, 7, and 8 weeks, before at last, one came and held on long enough, 'til the 39th week. We had to go to the hospital then, his one arm a bit weakened by the battle, and the cord wrapped three times preventing his safe passage out of the womb. A 4-inch incision brought him into the light. I am grateful for science, for C-Sections, for health care. I hate the word "miscarried," as if I had somehow done something terribly wrong.

That son went with me to the camp this summer, carried all the supplies in and out, built play structures and balloon animals. Over dinner at the Main Street Grill, he had me take the Political Compass Test. I was at the far edge of liberal beliefs. He told me he was a social libertarian and that he is grateful we allowed him to form his own ideology. I am reminded of the tuition we paid to the private Quaker elementary school, then the private Catholic middle school. He is at a large public high school now, enjoys art, science, and history. He wants to be a genetic engineer. I am proud of his wit and his compassion.

They say you grow into the face you deserve but I think karma is not so kind. She took both of George's lungs. Ed died choking on bile. I look toil-worn in the picture of me holding the child at camp. I have surrendered to the frizz of poorly conditioned curls, no longer fighting against excessive humidity. I have uncorrected wrinkles illustrating my décolletage and uneven skin tones revealing my haphazard application of sunscreen in my youth. What can I say? At least the wrinkles around my eyes are laugh wrinkles.

We are driving home on the country roads; I ease off the gas going into the curves, accelerate coming out. We have just stopped for peaches at the roadside market, and we will have them with ice cream once we get home.

My own teen, the one I had when I was 44, is arguing about politics with his friends on Instagram as we drive home from camp. He had loaded the car for me. We will take all the supplies back to the clinic, pack them away for next year—swings, switch-adapted light-up toys, pool noodles, stuffed animals weighted with fish gravel, and a gallon of bubble solution. My son turns to me and says, "I'm not for 3rd trimester abortions." I think of Cheri's child—he would be 45 now, old enough to win condoms at his own reunion. I think of the micro-preemie I just held, whose skin was so inflamed he could not play until calmed with deep pressure massage. I think of my pact with Mary; it seemed so reasonable at the time to step in front of a car rather than bear a bastard child. I think of lecherous English professors and vomit-covered pedophiles. I think of the small fetuses, lost at 4, 6, 6, 7, 7, & 8 weeks. I think of the wrinkles and the frizz that karma gifted me with in spite of all my prayers for straight, well-hydrated tresses. I ease off, breathe, let it pass. Karma is watching. I tell my son *"No one is,"* and accelerate out of another curve, *"no one is."*

Ecological Succession

by Matthew Ferrence

At the present rate it must come to pass
And that right soon that the meadow sweet
And steeple bush not good to eat
Will have crowded out the edible grass.

Then all there is to do is wait
For mop birch and spruce to push
Through meadow sweet and steeple bush
And crowd them out at a similar rate.

No plow among these rocks would pay
So busy yourself with other things
While the trees put on their wooden rings
And with long-sleeved broaches hold their sway.

Then cut down the trees when lumber grown,
And there's your pristine earth all freed
From lovely blooming but wasteful weed
And ready again for the grass to own.

A cycle we'll say of a hundred years.
Thus foresight does it and laissez faire,
A virtue in which we all may share
Unless a government interferes.

Patience and looking away ahead,
And leaving some things to take their course.
Hope may not nourish a cow or horse,
But spes alit agricolam 'tis said.

—Robert Frost, "Something For Hope"

Background Information:

Ecological Succession *refers to the sequential and orderly progression of communities that replace one another in a given area over time in response to changing environmental conditions. If the process begins from a barren situation that had not been previously inhabited, such as that found on a newly formed island or lava flow, the type of succession is classified as* **Primary Succession**. *If, for some reason, the progression is broken and set back to an earlier stage by some action of humans and/or nature, the type of succession is considered* **Secondary Succession**. *The first species to colonize an environment are commonly referred to as* **Pioneer Species**. *As environmental conditions change, these species are replaced by others that are better adapted to the new conditions. Eventually a community becomes established that maintains itself in a relatively stable relationship with its environment. This more stable community is referred to as the* **Climax Community**.

Procedure:

Begin with the regularly mowed area of field and progress into the forest. Divide the ecological communities encountered into six distinct stages: Mowed Grass, Wildflower, Shrub, Low Tree, Intermediate Tree, and Tall Tree. For each stage, make a list of characteristic plants and animals representative of that stage. Note any observable changes in abiotic factors. Note also the boundaries that separate each stage are not well-defined, but a gradual transition occurs from one stage to another. This necessitates that you focus attention on characteristic species rather than all species.

— *Gary M. Ferrence,* <u>Fundamentals of Environmental Biology</u>, *3rd Ed.*

What type of succession was studied? _____

    I grew up in, moved away from, and now live again in heavily forested Western Pennsylvania, within a state named specifically for the impressiveness of its trees: Penn's Woods. When William Penn gained the charter for the land from Charles II in 1681, more or less all of the colony's

29 million acres would have been dense, old-growth forest. By the end of World War I, heavy timbering had reduced the state's forest coverage to a low of 13 million acres, which has since recovered to 17 million acres. While a walk in these contemporary woods often passes by thick old trees and heavy undergrowth, the vast majority of even old-seeming forests are new growth. The ancient forests of the region long ago succumbed to farm clearing, timbering, and general development. Hardwoods like oak and chestnut were cleared in support of, first, the British economy and, later, a new America. Cleared land turned to pasture, and where farms failed or were abandoned, conifers took to the vacant grasslands. Those, too, were often felled, and the hardwoods grew once more in muddy, stumped clear-cuts, leading to the sort of mixed forest that now covers Pennsylvania and other heavily wooded sections of the Northeast.

Measured on the timeline of European activity in North America, sustained periods of clear-cutting tally in the order of two, but these ancient forests experienced perhaps countless cycles of change over their many years, in a process first named "succession" by French Naturalist Adolphe de la Malle in the 18th century. In tracking the way plants repopulated cleared forests, de la Malle recognized the seed of contemporary environmental science, which now recognizes the constant dynamism of natural landscapes. More simply, what I think of as "the woods," say the brambled slashing at the top of my parents' farm or the oak-filled squirrel hunting grounds on another nearby family acreage, is really a product of chance occurrences, random propagations, and often, recovery from various catastrophic events.

In Pennsylvania, only a handful of actual old growth remains, in a few contained patches of forest preserved by the timber companies either in uncommon recognition of the rapid destruction splintering at the axe, or perhaps, in a cagey preservation of high-dollar tight-grained old wood. Only in places like Hearts Content, not too far from my current home in Northwestern Pennsylvania, can a person walk among a reasonable version of the sort of forests that predated human consumption of wood. Here, the forest is marked by a more or less homogeneous vegetation, since these climax forests by definition contain low species diversity. Each member of the community is essentially perfectly suited to the environment at hand.

Defined somewhat imprecisely, inertia describes a universal and undeniable preference for stability. Succession, then, describes the boreal process of inertia. In the way forests repopulate themselves and build, once again, toward stasis, we see both a remarkable process of renewal and a disconcerting preference for rigidity.

How would this progression differ if you were in:

A. ~~Southern Arizona~~ Poland

Eventually we found the village, a scattered collection of ramshackle houses more or less nearby the church. "Village" suggests too much. The word evokes the alpine architecture of Zakopane, the tony ski resort just a few hours south. The word implies thatch, ruddiness, and nostalgic simplicity. From a distance, the draft horses we watched pull a wagon load of cut hay supported such a notion. Up close, the rusty satellite dishes planted in muddy front yards demonstrated that horses are, in fact, simply cheaper than cars.

Our driver leaned against the fender of his car, while my mother and I climbed into the hillside cemetery overlooking the church there in Niedzwiedz. She unfolded a piece of notepaper, checking the precise handwriting for names we hoped to find on gravestones. Her great-grandmother had been buried here long ago, before the Germans and before the Communists and before the old church had burned to the ground. We walked among the graves, earthen mounds here in Poland, six feet long, a couple feet wide, the bones lying not far beneath us. In some places, richer dead folk lay in concrete vaults surrounded by shining votives and silken flowers. In the older part of the graveyard, where we walked back and forth among the markers, we squinted to make out names on metal crosses, realizing that caustic rain had long since erased legibility.

Here, the paths were choked by weeds, and I sometimes tripped on the raised earth of unseen graves. It was soon clear that we'd not find what we'd come for. No one had been left to tend this grave, and so the weeds had done the job in their own way. My mother's grandmother had been sent away from her own mother in 1899, shipped off to Chicago when she was only fourteen in a Poland occupied, then, by empires from Prussia and Austria and Russia. The farmland had been destroyed, and the Poles were starving. This had been the best choice. Scrape together enough money to secure slow passage across the ocean, send a child away, where at least there might be a chance, where graves might at least be tended and not forgotten.

I had intended to leave a token in the graveyard, to lay a pencil on the grave of my great-great grandmother as recognition of the parts of her that I carried within myself. Instead, I crouched among the whorled roots of an old oak in the center of the graveyard, then pressed the pencil deep into the earth, where it would melt, eventually, into soil.

B. ~~Northern Canada~~ Slovakia

We'd been told the water was high, the river swollen by weeks of heavy summer rain. I expected white water, something far quicker than the slight current of this shallow flow. Instead, we sat in shallow wooden boats, each a series of flattened canoes lashed together. At the helm, a weathered Pole wore traditional costume for the benefit of the tourists in the boat. Periodically, he pressed a long staff into the gravel bottom and pressed the boat forward. Satisfied with our course, he squatted on the edge of the boat and plucked his burning cigarette from between the slats. He drew slowly, then offered clouds of smoke that drifted along the boat into our faces. Each cigarette diminished slowly, down to his fingertips until he flicked the butt between the boards of the raft, where it drowned in the Dunajec and floated beneath us. We drifted in that manner for two hours, slowly winding our way from one country to the other, repeatedly crossing the border between Slovakia and Poland, floating the division of my origins. My father took photos and remarked on the beauty of Slovakian churches. My mother sat quietly, drawing in the sheer faces of Polish rock carved by the steady rub of the river.

The day before, my father and I had walked that same border, higher up, toeing the rocks of a ten-foot path cut across the ridge at Kasprowy

Wierch. Creeping fog reduced a clear July afternoon to ethereal cloud, driving many mountaintop visitors to the ski lodge café and simply erasing the view of the rest. I watched my father lean into his walking stick. Polish ski slopes lay to our left, a thousand feet of Slovakian mountain valley to our right. He joked that he might just head that way, set off down the slope into the homeland and seek out lost cousins in Bratislava. Moments later, he spied a pink-purple wild flower just off the ridge top, maybe ten feet down into Slovakia. He pinned his walking stick between loose stones, hung on, bent over with his camera. While he teetered over the flower, I took my own photo—of him. If he lost his balance and slid into the chasm, at least I'd have a shot of his last moments.

How would this progression differ if you were in:

A. ~~Southern Arizona~~ ~~Poland~~ Pennsylvania

Not long ago, Wendell Berry traveled from his Kentucky farm for a rare public appearance at the college where I teach. As part of the kickoff for a sustainable forestry conference, Berry anchored a panel of experts on timber management. My father drove two hours from his own reclaimed farm, and the two of us snuck into an auditorium filled with an odd collection of timber men and women: pot bellied farmers; scruffy axemen; some hipster loggers wearing flannel, dirty work boots, and retro eyeglasses. My father urged me to the front row, where I felt old feelings of embarrassment flush. This was my turf, new turf, as I'd only joined this particular faculty nine months before, and in some ways I resented the ease at which I returned to the simple role of son, settling into the front row where he wanted to sit.

I counted Berry's appearance here as both miracle and gift. I had only recently started reading his work with a mature eye, while preparing to teach my environmental literature class. I'd been struck reading him, both by the utter majesty of his writing and by uncanny coincidence. The farm I grew up on had been my father's reclamation project, a choked hundred acres left behind when a developer lost his fortune in Vegas, not unlike the salvage job Berry had engaged in the south. I'm not sure why it came as such a surprise, then, when my father informed me that Berry was one of his and, particularly, one of my mother's favorite authors. That Berry so rarely travels for events like that conference barely factored into this calculus of shock.

But he had a friend in the area, another member of the panel in fact, who runs a forest conservancy founded on principles of sustainable timber management. So many people move away from our Pennsylvania woods; thus, so many inherit forests for which they have little use. Often, clear-cuts present a precise and rapid execution of the estate. The conservancy offers a different option: horse-driven timbering that includes careful, laborious selection of trees. As the panel made clear, they do not high-grade: this describes a responsible-sounding practice that, in reality, mows down all of the healthiest, most biologically robust trees and leaves the spindly weak stuff behind. The rhetoric of high-grading describes this as a way to give little trees a chance to grow stronger while, instead, such practice removes strong genetics from the gene pool and leaves only the weakest behind. As a forestry professor from Penn State described on the stage, such cutting is analogous to a dairy farmer slaughtering all of his good milkers to give the poor producers a chance to make more milk.

In adopting horses as timber vehicle, the conservancy also sought to protect the land from ruts, erosion, and the kind of ruptured soil that machines cannot avoid, thereby preserving the perpetual harvest of timber in much the same way Berry writes of redeeming sloped fields with horse-drawn plows in "The Making of a Marginal Farm." But suffice it to say, neither this timber conservancy nor Wendell Berry were proposing a human-free succession. Quite obviously, their forests are not being allowed to succumb to inertia. They are managed, held back from climax states by one of the chief ecological disturbances that ends so-called primary succession—the original process of development in a forest—and creates conditions favorable for secondary succession.

Viewed through the lens of the panel on that stage, and through that of my father as well, the presence of humans in the process of succession is less a disturbance than a partnership. Theirs are philosophies that seek to avoid the binary of environment versus human, that trumpet the merits of responsible use and human membership within the environ-ment itself. And, really, that strikes me as a prudent stance. As Lynn White, Jr. and many other ecological scholars have noted, the separation of human and nature is, in a sense, a pathology rooted within deeply-embedded Judeo-Christian concepts of natural dominion.

Perhaps the ideal forest is not one of climax, then, not one of rigid homogeneity, but a forest that makes room for human beings within the ecological exchange. We manage and are managed by forests. We are part of the forests, acting upon the environment to alter the balance, for sure, but allowing ourselves to also be acted upon by the environment to give us balance. Sustainability and ethics happen when we recognize both our position as part of ecology and that forest preservation like all environmentalism is really, at heart, self-preservation.

B. ~~Northern Canada~~ ~~Slovakia~~ Vermont

Parts of the Robert Frost Interpretive Trail, located in the Green Mountain National Forest near Ripton, Vermont, run alongside the South Branch of the Middlebury River, which drains water from Breadloaf Mountain into the farm valley below. Recently, I walked that trail with a small group led by John Elder, a retired professor from nearby Middlebury College. Poles flank the trail at irregular intervals, upon which are fastened Robert Frost poems, some famous and some less so. Visitors walk the landscape described in the poems, and in some small way have a chance to gain different perspectives into a body of literature that, too often, loses power through its familiarity.

On that walk, John described the process of the land we observed: how a pond that had not too many years ago been open and that is now filling in with bog plants had been so changed by the washout of a beaver pond; how Forestry Service crews periodically mow and torch the shrubs that take root in the meadows beside the trail; and how the wide barrens below spruce trees are secured by the tannic acids released by the trees themselves, who secure their fortune by poisoning away other botanical competitors.

The idea of the trail, John explained, was to allow visitors to see the Vermont that Frost would have seen, to in some small way fix in time the stages of Frost's landscape. Nature rarely allows such grooming without a fight, of course, a fact clear enough from the river. Just a year before this walk, Hurricane Irene pounded up the East Coast, flooding into Vermont with a rare inland fury. The force of water rushing down so many mountain streams ripped banks away, knocked trees asunder, even re-carved the channel in many places in many waterways. The evidence of that disturbance is clear enough on the South Branch, where what not long ago would have been just a gentle stream is now a gentle stream flanked by wide expanses of large gravel and sheer mud cliffs. Uprooted trees litter the banks in places, and it's not hard to be amazed at the sheer volume of water that must have coursed through this place.

A day before the walk, I sat on the grassy lawn in front of Frost's nearby writing cabin while John addressed a group of writers gathered for the Breadloaf Writers Conference. While the intense August sun quickly doused rivulets from my neck and back, John gracefully stood under a sugar maple and described the forest history of Vermont. With the exception of the Upper Peninsula of Michigan, he explained, no part of the United States was timbered more thoroughly than Vermont. While the state seems to exist in a gloried, untouched, pristine state of forest, it in fact has been clear-cut—to bare earth—twice. First went the hardwood, felled for potash and charcoal, cleared away for farms. When the farms failed, in grew the conifers, which were ripped free, and just like in my own Pennsylvania, the contemporary mixed forest finally grew in.

In a section of Mountains of Home fittingly called "Succession," Elder writes of the 100-year-long cycles through which old farm fields grow back into forests. This cycle "offers redemptive visions of inclusiveness," he suggests. "There is a grand logic of transformation, meaningful to the thoughtful observer, but always transcending the limited human purposes with which we might identify one phase or another of the whole." In a way, Elder speaks softly against the notion of the human control of the environment. Such an enterprise is hardly more than hubris, revealed in the folly of clearing Vermont mountains to plant farms in a glaciated landscape devoid of topsoil. There can be no human control in such a situation, since the action of farming fails to recognize the capacity of the land. Control, here, is illusory, a fantasy of domination wrecked by the relentless desire of forest to be forest.

I think of these words when I think about the eroded banks of the South Branch, where the glacial till has been laid bare by the powerful forces of tropical weather. I've always been drawn to water, moving and still, fresh or salt. And even in its torrents, I've never quite been able to muster anger. Instead, I recall wonder and excitement when the stream in our lower pasture used to bubble muddy gushes after summer thunderstorms. At normal levels, that small stream offered a perfect site for childhood wading and crayfish catching, but in the storms its capacity breached the banks, spread across the flat edges of the pasture, bypassed the corrugated steel culverts the gas drilling company had installed to keep their access road intact.

That's a redemption to me, that alone. Maybe three times a summer, the tiny stream refused to submit to the gas company's will, something my father could never avoid doing, thanks to subsurface rights controlled by a long gone, out-of-state former owner. Water finds its own course, as it did in our Pennsylvania pasture, and as it so clearly did in the South Branch of the Middlebury River. Water is perpetual, and so too, its frictions. The storms of Irene knocked out power for weeks, collapsed roads for months, and wreaked havoc on the state in ways that were, no doubt, difficult and painful for residents to deal with.

But looking down the South Branch, feet on the wooden bridge over the water, listening to John recall a story of guiding the Dalai Lama on that very trail, he senses the fallen trees on the bank evoke something other than despair. "A fallen log is something for hope," he writes in "Succession," "A hope, rather, for involvement in the grand pattern that connects."

How would this progression differ if you were in:

A. ~~Southern Arizona~~ ~~Poland~~ ~~Pennsylvania~~ Chicago

My mother grew up in Gary, Indiana, the daughter of a Chicago postman and an elementary school secretary. Her father golfed and drank too much. Likely for one of these reasons, my grandmother sent her away to a boarding school in South Bend. At St. Mary's, my mother met the Notre Dame boys, even went to one of their formals with Perry Como's son. After high school, my mother moved to Chicago's St. Xavier College, then into the second grade classrooms of Kokomo, later to Monroe County, where she worked with the students who struggled the most. One of them, sixteen years old and still yet to learn to read, presented my mother with a bag of persimmons from her backyard tree. Suspicious of the pungency of the fruit and the dripping juice seeping through the bag, my mother worried about a connection between the decay of the students' school clothes and general rot. My mother thanked the student before secretly tossing the persimmons in the school incinerator. As she turned away from the flames, she saw the girl wave from a passing school bus. My mother has always wondered how much or how little the girl understood about the guilt of that moment, when her own failure to understand the ripeness of persimmons may or may not have meant so much.

B. ~~Northern Canada~~ Slovakia ~~Vermont~~ Summit Station

My father grew up in an Eastern Pennsylvania whistle-stop village. Never prosperous, the family ran the local general store, where he pumped gas and dropped nickels into their bootleg slot machine. His father ran shovel at an open-pit anthracite mine, spent large periods of my father's childhood living away from home during the work week. When anthracite demand plummeted after World War II, his father took odd jobs around Summit clearing brush or selling chickens or cutting trees. Never prosperous, his father boxed under the ring name "Farmer John," earning greasy dollars by exploiting his natural talent for absorbing punches, if not the talent for landing them. My father's uncle picked up the trash at nearby Fort Indiantown Gap, locally called "The Gap." His uncle plucked fraying fatigues from the refuse, gave them to my grandmother, who patched the holes and gave them to my father as school clothes. Never prosperous, my father ate the persimmons that grew on his grandparents' tree. Never prosperous, my father learned fast that his Pennsylvania Dutch accent led only to jeers from students and teachers, who, in this already hard-up part of Pennsylvania, understood the accent as the mark of someone, at least, poorer than them.

How would this progression differ if you were in:

A. ~~Southern Arizona~~ ~~Poland~~ ~~Pennsylvania~~ ~~Chicago~~

Southern Arizona

Just east of our house, earth-moving equipment made short work of the desert. Thickets of mesquite, ocotillo, cholla, and prickly pear mounded into heaps ready for burning. Plumes of black diesel exhaust scoured giant blades across the earth, exposing red desert. My wife and I lived, then, in Sierra Vista, a small city that grew out of the brothels that used to flank Fort Huachuca, home of the Buffalo Soldiers. Now, the fort serves as a communications and intelligence proving ground for the Army, and seedy old Fry Town has grown into 40,000-strong Sierra Vista.

As with all desert towns, growth and sprawl are indistinguishable: new homes pop up south and east, cutting away the desert to make way for pseudo-adobe houses. In the former desert just east of our old neighborhood—which itself had been carved out of the shrub around the time of my birth in the dead center of the 70s—foundations appeared quickly, sprouting from the earth much like forest mushrooms sprout on rotting logs in the Pennsylvania woods. Crews worked quickly, and frames sprang up, followed by sheathing, followed by stucco. Inside, the plumbers and electricians spun the systems, followed by the sheetrockers, then crews of finish carpenters who tacked on the moldings and trim. Houses appear there as if in time-lapse films. Crews remove the desert, then head to the next place.

Just beyond this new development, barbed wire demarcated the end of development. Signs declared it property of the local water authority. A dry gulch wound through that part of the landscape, a small chasm of dust and rocks for most of the year. During summer, however, thunderstorms build over the Huachuca Mountains, and on most afternoons hard rain floods the draw. Water runs thick, the ocotillo bloom, and desert drab becomes a truer shade of green. After the rains, frog song emerges, along with flowers, and life, and all that makes the desert much more than a wasteland.

For a housing development, such action in water proves inconvenient. The draws are converted to culverts. The rushing flow of desert water is diverted into proper channels, redefined as wastewater.

B. ~~Northern Canada~~ ~~Slovakia~~ ~~Vermont~~ ~~Summit Station~~ Paris

On the first day, I was tired. By the second, I was scared, here in this new home where the language failed me and where the horizon disappeared behind layers of Parisian architecture. I became lost, or perhaps finished my journey into lost. I came to Paris this way: as an obedient child and quiet student who declined the prestigious college where my mother used to dance to enroll in the local one, because free tuition was one of my father's professional perks. A communications major becomes a biology major becomes a music major becomes a business major becomes a physics major becomes a music major again becomes an English major. Add an M.F.A. from the city down the road, then write for a newspaper, start teaching for a college, quit for a desert Ph.D., quit again three months in, earn $400 aggregate as a freelance writer, move to Paris so my wife can finish her own master's.

I came to Paris this way also: as a 28-year-old who had always chosen the path of least resistance. My great rebellions in life had been majoring in English and spending a college fund not spent on college to bankroll living in Paris. I wonder, now, ten summers after my first in France, if the terror I then called culture shock was better described as growing up.

At 66 rue d'Alleray, I lived without a target, and targets function for the mind very much as a safety net functions for the man on the wire. Targets imply path, are the destination of properly applied rationality, the clear and undeniable motion toward success. This, in Paris, was what I had given away. I had no particular aim, only nebulous ideas of writing and golf. Neither of these professions offered much hope of independent success, let alone stability. And, as it turned out, my career as a professional golfer amounted to half a dozen last-place finishes and career earnings of minus five thousand dollars.

In the language of ecological succession, "disturbance" is defined as a "temporary change in average environmental conditions." For a forest, disturbances include invasive species, flooding, logging, fire, and windthrow. It is this last term, I think, that describes my early moments of despair in Paris, when I lay in bed at night sobbing for some hard-felt loss, terrified of the days that lay ahead of me. In the forest, windthrow describes the periodic uprooting of trees knocked down by wind, itself a force visible only by its effect: lightly fluttering drapes, or desk papers whisking in a sudden gust, or the cyclonic dust devils of Arizona, or the sheared away tree that glistens wet after a summer thunderstorm. I was felled in Paris, blown to France by gentle winds of desire, by love for my wife, by dissatisfaction with the choices I hadn't made. I was uprooted in Paris, befuddled by the disorientation of facing a life governed only by my choices.

How would this progression differ if you were in:

A. ~~Southern Arizona~~ ~~Poland~~ ~~Pennsylvania~~ ~~Chicago~~
~~Southern Arizona~~ Paris

When my father visited us in Paris, he and I visited the Musée de le Chasse et de la Nature, and I've long wondered why a moment from that trip lingers within me, frequently calling out as if to say, "this is important." We went because my father loves hunting and nature, the specific charge of that museum. But at the end of our tour, we turned into a small room filled with oil paintings of laundry blowing in the breeze. This was a random installation, some exhibit outside the usual scope of the Musée. Several of the city's museums had rooms like this that summer, space set aside for contemporary artists to show their work.

I remember the bulk of the museum as dusty, quiet in a moldering sort of way. Bald spots shone through many of the taxidermy mounts on display. I remember the paintings of laundry as fluttering in my heart, some breeze at that moment separating what I valued in the museum, perhaps, from what my father valued, even though everything of value lay under the same verse. The exhibit staked its own claim in a new habitat of artistic self-definition. The artwork fit, not because it was of the same subject as the rest of the Musée, but because its presence expanded the scope of the place.

Jozef Paczoski, a Polish ecologist who wrote in Slavic, died the year my father was born, in 1941. Among his achievements was an early understanding of the way plants affect their own surroundings, that they are not merely subject to the land they are born into. Instead, through various mechanisms, they shape their environment, make it for themselves.

As a child of both Polish and Slavic heritage, I'm drawn to think of these ideas as somehow embedded within me, though I'd like to think also they are embedded within all of us. This is the potential that lay within my moment among laundry paintings in an obscure Parisian museum. In some way, the moment of vision, when these fluttering sheets appeared around a corner, was prepared for by the departing Polish and Slovakian children of my ancestry. This, I think, at least partly explains the resonance of that moment. As Paczoski understood, an organism can affect its own place within a community. An individual can alter the trajectory of succession, even long after the process has begun. Hidden winds fluttered those paintings, and the breeze wrapped around some spot inside of me, too.

B. ~~Northern Canada~~ Slovakia ~~Vermont Summit Station~~ ~~Paris~~ Vermont

Midway through the walk around the Robert Frost Trail, John Elder stopped beside a marker bearing the words of the poet's famous "Stopping By Woods on a Snowy Evening." The day had been sublime so far, a clarified blue sky, low humidity, pleasantly warm. Around Breadloaf, I had just the day before noticed the first tinges of scarlet on a few low branches, and already the crisp nights felt very much like autumn at home. The walk, too, had been nothing short of wonderful. John's gentle demeanor combined with his prodigious intellect to produce the quiet force of truth. He spoke of Frost in ways I was unaccustomed, redeeming him for me with a certain simplicity of purpose. Frost was a great observer of nature, John told us, and ecologically spot on. I suppose, for me, this rediscovery of Frost echoed what John writes in "Aji" about his own study of Vermont natural history, that "good things have come in roundabout and unanticipated ways." I should mention this, too: my father likes Robert Frost, perhaps the only poet he might choose to read for pleasure.

There we stood, at the halfway point, beside the marker, while John described a group of Vermonters reciting the famous poem aloud while traveling with groups from several other nations. He invited my own group to do so, and more than a few knew the poem well enough to oblige in the choral reading. And as surprised as I might have been by their memories—I wasn't able to muster the words to speak alongside them—I was more surprised to find my throat catching near the end of the poem, when the speaker's horse

> . . . gives his harness bells a shake
> to ask if there is some mistake.
> The only other sound's the sweep
> Of easy wind and downy flake.

The group finished, and I looked ahead at the peak of the distant ridge. We stepped forward, then stopped again soon near a clearing populated by wild berries. John described how bears will settle into such patches, hunker down and take mighty sweeps with the paws until every last berry has been consumed. And there, in that moment, suddenly, I felt myself as a child, walking behind a stream of college students, my father at the helm explaining this biological function or that, pausing beside a stream, boot on a rock in that fashion I know so well. I could hear my father's voice, a projecting authority, not without tenderness, as he pinched a caddis fly nymph between his fingers and explained the life cycle, how the young changes over time into the adult, who in turn provides young for another generation.

I lagged behind the group on the Frost Trail, my composure slipping. I felt my eyes well up, flooded from what, in the moment, was an unidentifiable sense of significance. I thought of my father, and in the next moment of my son, Jozef, of walking trails together. I thought of the salve of walking, the succor of Thoreau's wilderness, of how much my son has loved to walk since he learned how. He tracked circles around and around and around our house, reaching his arms into my hands and declaring, "Daddy, walk." Daddy, walk. Daddy, walk, indeed, the succession of myself as the son who walked with his father, who will continue to walk with his father, who will be the father who walks with his son, who somehow on that August afternoon walked with both, who were each 500 miles away.

"A fallen log is something for hope," John Elder writes, and I wonder now about the infinite regression of fallen logs, fertile spaces that litter forests, literal and imagined. The best promises we can keep are to make space for such logs, always, to walk among them when we can. And I know, too, that the making of such space is the true nature of inertia. It is the source of real stability, that of our world and our own lives. I do not wonder about the infinite regression of hope. I am convinced by John Elder, and Frost, and my father, and by the stories of ancestors who sought to change their family lot by boat and by degree. I am convinced that we walk always in forests alongside those who came before us.

Feathered Roach Clips and Goldfish

by Karen J. Weyant

Sitting on her front porch banister, Kimmy and I watched the older neighborhood girls walk towards the carnival grounds. Wearing t-shirts and Jordache jeans with their long-strapped purses carelessly thrown over their shoulders, they strode by us, confident in their pursuit of a good time at our town's biggest social event of the summer.

Every year, in our small Pennsylvanian town, we had been forlorn witnesses as the town got ready for the annual Volunteer Firemen's Carnival. And every year, we had to wait patiently for our parents, grandparents, or a favorite aunt or uncle to take us. Once there, they would hover over us, monitoring what we ate and steering us away from what they deemed inappropriate or "too scary" carnival rides.

But this year, everything was different. This year, we were finally old enough to go to the carnival on our own.

We had scrimped and saved our money for this week, and we were ready. We were ready to ride the Paratroopers, our feet dangling beneath the safety bars at death-defying heights. We were ready to spin around in the Tilt-a-Whirl until our stomachs and heads both twirled. We were ready for sticky fingers from fried dough and caramel apples, any treat that we usually couldn't have as they would spoil our suppers.

Obviously, now that we were on our own, there would be no proper meals, so we didn't need to worry about spoiling our appetites.

And we were ready to take part in the newest carnival trend. Every year, during a week, a new carnival fad invaded our small town. One year, pairs of fuzzy dice were the fad. Another year, there were stretch Coke bottles filled with bright colors of liquid. For a few years now, painted logos of rock bands on mirrors, were also becoming collectibles.

This year, the girls were all wearing feathered roach clips, and somehow, I had scored two of these accessories from a neighbor who had somehow acquired quite a collection in just the one night she had been at the carnival. However, I had a feeling that the two clips she gave me were mere castoffs as one was bright pink and had a cracked bead while the other one was made out of dull brown feathers.

I gave Kimmy the pink feathered clip, as I pulled back strands of my hair with the other one. We examined ourselves in the full-length mirror found in her mother's bedroom. We rearranged strands of hair, took the clips out, reclipped. We knew we could get better clips at the carnival—perhaps ones with striped feathers or sparkly beads.

But we both knew we wanted more than just our own feathered roach clips.

We wanted to win our own goldfish.

Goldfish were everywhere during carnival week. Swimming alone in clear plastic bags filled with water, they stared out at the world around them. They swung from the handles of bicycles and the tight fists of children as they took home their treasures: real animals that were way better than any other carnival prize.

Once the feathered clips were in place, we tucked our money deep into our pockets and walked to the carnival grounds. Once we arrived, we stood in wonder as grandparents crowded into large tents to play Bingo, and girls walked around with teddy bears tucked under their arms, prizes from boyfriends who knocked over milk bottles or shot thin cardboard duck targets with pellet guns. Fried food smells filled the air, and music vibrated through the grounds. Yes, we had seen this world before, but now, free from adult supervision, we viewed the scene in front of us with fresh and eager eyes.

We had a strategy in place for our evening. First, we would walk around and decide what carnival rides would be the most fun. Then, we would examine the games and eat some not-so-good-for-us food. We would try to find some roach clips of our own. And for the most part, we followed this strategy, with both of us deciding that we had outgrown the bumper cars, but the Ferris Wheel, especially when we rocked our cart at the top when the ride stalled, was still one of our favorites.

But then, we forgot the roach clips, even with our hand-me-down clips tangled in our hair. Perhaps it was because we spotted the tent with the goldfish.

To win a goldfish, we needed to throw a ping-pong ball into a small round bowl of water. Chances of winning were good—especially for two eight-year-olds who couldn't throw darts hard enough to pop a balloon or understand the strategies of a Bingo card. Kimmy won hers right away and stood behind me clutching her prize while waiting patiently. Still, it took me a few tries (and quite a few quarters) before I finally succeeded, and a burly, gruff-voiced man handed me my own goldfish tucked safely in a plastic bag.

I cradled the plastic bag and stared at the small fish inside. The fish stared back, its tiny scales catching the carnival lights.

We started our walk home, hands clasping the bags. We talked about possible names of our fish and Kimmy wasn't very imaginative, saying she would call hers Goldie.

My fish had small black dots on its fins. "I think I'm going to name mine Speckles," I told her.

We then discussed the future homes for our fish. Kimmy had a small bowl in her bedroom that she was sure was going to work. However, I had something better. A few years ago, my mother had kept an aquarium full of fish. Once the fish had died, she never bothered replacing them, so after cleaning out the aquariums, she stored it in the attic. I just knew that my goldfish would be happy swimming in a much bigger place. It was common knowledge that the prized goldfish rarely lived very long after traveling to their prospective homes. My friends had told me stories of waking up to feed their pets and finding them belly side up in the water. Plus, common sense dictated that having a cat in the household would also affect a pet goldfish's survival rate. Still, I had heard stories of some goldfish who grew as big as fists and others that got too big for their homes so they were released in ponds.

As we walked, we talked about strategies for our new pets' survival. The night was warm and muggy and soon, the lights from the carnival ground faded. The feather roach clips slipped slowly from our hair, and somewhere between Chestnut Avenue and Cherry we lost them.

But we didn't care.

We both had our goldfish. I was sure that my new pet would not only survive but thrive.

POETRY

My personal connection to Northern Appalachia runs deep, as I was born and raised seven miles northeast of Wheeling, WV, in the hills above the Ohio River. Wheeling, like so many of the industrial river towns up and down the Ohio, has experienced its times of prosperity and decline, and its landscape and culture represent some of the great contradictions of the region. I never came to understand the valley and its culture as different from anywhere else until I was able to apply the perspectives of experience and adulthood toward where I am from. And now, as I reflect on that process while writing this introduction, I can visualize my personal journey through a multitude of literary landscapes that were always, whether I knew it or not, leading me on a path toward home. It just took me a while to find my way back.

Early in my reading life, I had always been drawn to works that conveyed that strong sense of place, ones in which the setting is almost a character, and if it had a map in the front pages, even better. I traveled to Faulkner's Yoknapatawpha County, Tolkien's Middle-earth, Twain's St. Petersburg, Anderson's Winesburg, and then on to Frost's New England, Masters' Spoon River, Robinson's Tilbury Town, and the list could go on. All these stories and poems in some way conveyed an intense search for an understanding of home. But these were all such far-away places for an Ohio Valley kid like me.

And then it happened. I was pursuing my PhD at Indiana University of Pennsylvania and struggling to settle on a subject for my dissertation until I signed up for a seminar in Modern American Poetry. Flipping through the pages of an anthology, searching for a topic for a paper, I came across a poem I had read once long ago, but because of the inexperience of youth, it had never really stuck. A little twelve-line poem that took me straight from Indiana, PA, right back to the valley, the factories, the mills, the river, the modest houses up and down its banks, and the men and women and children living, working, and dreaming there. The poem was titled "Autumn Begins in Martins Ferry, Ohio," by James Wright.

It had been more than fifteen years since I had read or even thought about that poem. But what struck me as so true this time around was how the poem captured the struggle and pain, and at the same time the beauty and joy of the place—my place, my childhood, my growing up, my sense of home. It is in many ways the perfect Northern Appalachian poem, illustrating the extreme contradictions characteristic of the region—the industrial river valleys, full of natural beauty and at the same time pocked with the scars of industry, the blighted ruins of steel mills countered by the rolling hills and farmlands, the dream of escape to something better, and at the same time the deep-rooted reverence for home.

That encounter with Wright's poem marks the moment I decided I wanted to try to be a poet, the moment I realized I could write about where I was from, my native ground, my "little postage stamp of native soil," as Faulkner famously called his hometown. I went on to center my dissertation around the poetry of place, focusing on poets from various regions of the United States, including a chapter on Wright's Ohio poems. The point of this short personal narrative is this: I have always been drawn to poems and stories that strive to define and negotiate the authors' or characters' native ground, works that develop, define, and shape our ideas about how we inhabit places, and that is the guiding principle for this selection of poems.

In his essay "Buckeye," Scott Russell Sanders writes, "For each home ground we need new maps, living maps, stories and poems, photographs and paintings, essays and songs. We need to know where we are, so that we may dwell in our place with a full heart." Poetry, specifically that which is rooted firmly in place, can provide more fully these new kinds of maps that allow us to see and understand places and the people and cultures that inhabit them. It is this impulse that has guided the selection of these pieces and their organization.

As the process for assembling these poems took shape, I realized that, following Sander's notions, these poems could construct a new kind of map, charted from the places where the individual poets either are from or are writing about. As such, the selections have been organized geographically from the eastern-most portions of the region in Pennsylvania and southern New York, through central Pennsylvania, and on to Pittsburgh, picking up at the confluence of the Ohio. From there the poems follow the southwest flow of the Ohio watershed into West Virginia, to Appalachian Ohio, and ultimately end at the southeastern most portion of the region in Cincinnati. If readers choose to read through the poems from first to last, they will be roughly charting a course through the Northern Appalachian bioregion and its cultural landscapes from eastern Pennsylvania to southeastern Ohio.

Along with following this poetic map through the region, readers will find in these poems several of the fundamental characteristics that make Northern Appalachia both part of and distinct from the greater region—a reverence for the natural world, the rivers, hills and rolling farmlands, love of and influence of family, nostalgia, loss, blue-collar-steel-town culture, the daunting presence of industry and industrial ruins, struggle, and pain, but also the joy and the beauty of living, the love of life and culture and home. All of the poets collected here bring their own lived experience in the region to the page and have shared part of their "little postage stamp of native soil" to help construct this new poetic map of Northern Appalachia, a map that strives to fulfill our journal's mission to provide a literary identity and voice to the writers of this region, landscape, and culture, which we all love and live in so fully.

—William Scott Hanna, Poetry Editor

Northern Appalachia Review – Poetry

Elizabeth Solsburg

In my mother's house

Thunder growls low over these hills—
I had forgotten how storms here sneak

over the ridges to catch you
unprotected and unaware.

Though I have not thought of it for years,
in its echoes I can hear

your father's voice telling me it is the sound of angels bowling.
We were on the porch swing

where you later rocked my babies,
and he was counting beats between flash and roar

with his old rose-gold watch that spun
loose around his fine, thin bones.

I have it now, tucked away in boxes
along with my childhood.

I have kept the Sunday-dinner china,
your rosary

and a red lace jacket your mother wore once to a dance—
in a photograph when people lived only in black and white.

Also, the crystal glasses we lifted high to catch each new year's
good luck—just until this year, when it all spilled out onto your floor.

But no one wanted the piles of newspapers you'd saved
so I burned them in your yard,

whispered prayers into the fire,
watched them rise like incense to the cloudless sky,

then got into my car
to drive far from these hills

to the flat land, where you can see
the storms coming for miles.

Astronomy

Matt leans back and measures
himself against the swath of galaxy
scrolling above his busy world.

Wind off the constellations
claps tears onto his cheeks.

Fingers from impossible distances
tug at his gut until he has to blink
back the surge of nausea.

As the night wiffles about his sleep,
dark infinities disorder his sight.

Tomorrow again the routine,
coffee, the office, a bar, glimpses
of skin, all the clever decorum,

yet his eyes will feel something
like pockets rolled inside out.

Wash

Never so spontaneous I don't
take off my shoes, and here
I stand calf-deep in a creek,
shirtless, the current sporting
pebbles and sand across my toes.

I would roll back the water
like a blanket and plunge abed,
let the well-black, boreal-cold
sheet cover me, have it sting away
all the mug of dilating afternoons,
and even, come winter, flay all
feeling from this body, these bones.

Dead Water Deities

I hike rails deep into a cold hollow crease of the Kittatinny Ridge
where I build a railbed-gravel fire, warming plunge pool psalms
of cloudy sunset stains as trout shoot under schist ledges.

I pray to these dead water deities, water gods lost
to coal and pyrite that have returned and reclaimed
  this rusted ravine.

Deadwood burns a life of light and heat into ash
like these hills once burst into fire and smoke as machines
pierced and gouged and scraped a landscape interrupted.
Now woods sing in winds old ballads of bones creaking
in rivers, of saints butchered under floods.

Fires die floods recede, but the rhythms of these rails
and abandoned totems gather into eddies of song,
  chants for the gods of a new world,
   native brook trout that survived in headwaters,
  wild browns that have migrated from big rivers,
    the seeds of a rewilding.

Michael Garrigan

It's Just the Moon.

It wasn't long ago we could just
turn on our faucet and drink.
Straight out of the garden hose, even.

But then a few new roads cut across
the far ridge and bright lights started to shine
in dark oak woods. Well pads. I used to be able to see
the Milky Way more nights than not. But now, just the moon.

And now I get stuck behind diesel and 18 wheels on my way
to work down valley with the road crew. We get to repair
more potholes and install more guardrails. It's good money
and I only have to take off when the hard freeze settles in
which is only a few days a year usually in February, not for those
long four months December through March like before. No.
Just a few days. Just the moon and me on those nights I have off.

But then our water turned brown a few months back and it smelled
like an old wool work shirt stuck behind a radiator and now I spend
my Saturdays when I'm not working road crew filling jugs. I even
installed a gravity feed system so I can fill that large container I
have on the outside of the house so we can take clean showers.

I thought we were just drinking water,
but it was full of radon and arsenic
and now it's harder to sleep.

We have to close the blinds and pray it's just the moon.

Post-Industrial Wilderness, Rejoice!

I propose a Post-Industrial Wilderness designation
    where we sing hymns of abandoned
    collieries slowly decaying into rocky
    soil strewn with concrete and shovels.

Let us call these corrugated hillsides Wilderness!
    Let us rejoice in rust!

Let us rejoice in the stutter step cadence
of walking rail ties that lead into headwaters
trickling out of mine shafts covered by hemlock.
Let us place limestone back into the water,
an offering, a prayer of reclamation.

Let us hail this river that was once alive then killed
and now is burnt orange but thriving with wild trout
and there, that's a midge fluttering above the neon oily
sheen but that's life, that's resilience, that's wildness
returning and spreading and goddamn! that's beautiful!

Let us bulldoze the dams! Let water run wild again!
Let it grow, all of it, even the invasives!
    Let knotweed arc over thistle and beer can.
For what is native in a place that has been scraped
and curled by furnace blasts?

Let us lay in the debris of our consumption
and smile when we feel worms between our toes,
glass shard pushing into the back of our calf,

a plastic lid crinkling under our fourth rib
a cement wall in the kink of our neck
a fleck of neon light that never stops
shimmering in our eyelash.

Let the earth swear at us
Let us love these curse words
Let them become sacred
lines, holy prayers that heal
the cracks of our destruction.

Let us rejoice in the harmony of mountain laurel and anthracite!

Let us rename this slag heap with signs
marking the boundaries of the abandoned:

Post-Industrial Wilderness
      Let it Grow.

Their Spring Best

You ride into town via the state highway, fading off from a few hundred miles of trailer trucks and cars that paced and chased you all the while. First you go to your mother's house, eat dinner. Your mother mentions an article in the paper last week about kids you went to high school with who were in a bad accident on a country road. Says she saw a girl you dated for a while senior year working at the new drugstore up in the plaza. You barely knew those kids in the car wreck, can't say you were friends with them. The girl you'd like to forget, but acknowledge the mention of her, largely in silence, replying with nods and looks. By dark you're past restless and so take your leave, walk uptown. You hit the usual places, but the usual places are no longer used to you. Things change, even in a quick year or two. But it is not until the third bar that you fully sense the turn. The bartender, a guy a few years older who likely never travels more than ten miles from home, won't accept your military ID until Petey White, who you worked with on a summer job a few years back, vouches for you. The place is crowded. Voices and heavy metal jukebox music all meld together. You scan the faces, head toward a group of old neighborhood kids, half of them underage, which makes you think again about the carding policy. And even though you aren't tight with them because they were always somebody's younger brother or sister, you go talk to those kids because it is better than standing alone like a jackass. After a few minutes, a guy you should recognize accidentally on purpose bumps into you, honchos his way between you and a girl with frizzy blonde hair. You can feel his tension so you turn to the guy, realize he is one of the Faust brothers. You know who he runs with, and tell him your name and mention your cousin-brother's name because he used to run with those guys too. But he curses your cousin-brother and you ask him not to, but he does it again, with a grin. You hit him with a brown fist that lands solid hard on his cheek, knocks him back a bit. These days you are quick to anger and quick to react because these days you have slowly begun to comprehend the complexity of the trick that has been played on you. It will take years before you fully figure what's what and do with that what you can. But in that moment, you give your best fake hard stare to the Faust kid's friends who are not sure whether to come after you and then head toward the door with the bartender screaming behind that you are banned for life. Outside, you slip into an alley, sit on someone's steps, catch your breath a minute until the night chill envelops you. You smoke cigarettes and walk directionless for the next few hours. You do not head home until you find yourself up on the hill at the intersection of Race and Line streets and notice a car filled with Christians, dressed in their spring best, on their way to Easter sunrise service.

Almost

You are fifteen and riding a motorcycle on rain-wet county roads in the middle of Pennsylvania. It is the kind of activity that brings a state trooper to a mother's door while neighbors look on, wondering what's the matter. Your cousin, who you will soon learn is really your half-brother, is fourteen and riding with you. He is on his stepfather's 305 Honda Scrambler with a purple metal flake tank and trim. You have the blue 250 Yamaha Enduro. Earlier you and your cousin crossed a long and narrow bridge, did a half loop around the traffic circle carefully dodging the tractor trailers, and headed up and over Blue Hill. At the bottom of the hill, just across the county line, lives a girl who has called your cousin on the telephone a few times. It was his idea to take the bikes and go see her, but once there he only talks to her for a few minutes and then he and you head away.

Years later you will see this girl in a bar near closing time with a guy who is stumbling drunk. He clings to her like property. She tries to talk to you, to recall that day years ago. You ghost-look her, then walk away because you are not interested because she belongs to a different time, a different place, a time that seems disconnected from the current moment. Of course, everything is connected, even those who are reading this here and now. When you are on the motorcycle riding on the rain-wet pavement you feel good for a moment, relaxed and away from the world. Then you try to take a curve a little too fast going downhill and the wheels lock up and you skid into the wrong lane. You are headed for a tree: a wide, sturdy oak and you think that you will hit it and that you will die. You think maybe you did die. Maybe everything that came after that moment is an illusion. Perhaps the world is only poorly reasoned assumptions and a tissue of lies. And you think that maybe to hit that tree would have been the best possible outcome. But you didn't. You downshifted, rode the curve, and moved on to survive other hills in the years that followed, some by accident and some on purpose.

Milky Way Above, Marcellus Shale Below

Many things wake me in the deep night,
but the best is the great horned owls
calling to each other beyond the mesh
of summer's window. My husband and I
first heard them January after we moved in,
pausing at the back door to stare at stars
in cold so sharp I thought the dark might crack
from lovers' need to reach across it.

Warm nights now they're joined by crickets
and the thrilling whine of coyotes—
brush wolves folks once called them here.
The men who built this house at the end
of our war against ourselves
stood in the cupola and looked for Indians.
Now, in every direction, they'd see
the Marcellus Borealis highlighting the hills
from well pads tucked in tight below.
To the south, a faraway drill rig
gives us on our front porch
the white-lighted finger.

Before bed the other night,
when I let my dog out, the backyard—
garden, chickens, meadows, woods—
all were frozen beneath the galaxy's shattering,
and I thought, *You can't touch this.*
You just can't.

Lilace Mellin Guignard

After The Magi Depart

On the tongue the names sparkle like snowflakes—
benzene, toluene, xylene—
before their sounds melt into air.
Parents watching kids leap and tumble in white drifts
would need to repeat the syllables to keep them
from evaporating, but who doesn't want fear
to break into tiny pieces and float away?

So of course we focus on the children
sledding down and trudging up the hill,
nothing around but cow pastures, corn fields,
fences, and a drill rig flaring half-mile away,
the tip cozy like a candle.

This is the life, the land, we know.
Change is coming. We can feel it
like a dream and squint into the twilight
looking for our kids, looking for a sign
clear as an angel saying,
"Arise, and take the young child . . ."

But all we hear is *benzene, toluene, xylene*.
The air is crisp and sparkles.
Our children laugh through blue lips.

Tattoo

Mount Saviour Monastery, February 2020

The pasture snow is bright as an unmarked page
as I saunter past after a morning at the desk.
Fir trees in the distance could be a chorus
line of nuns in crisp white habits,
or anything else I might imagine. Except

dead ahead, on my right, I see the frenzied
jerking of a deer, her bleeding hind leg caught
between fence wires. My soothing words as I climb
the snow bank don't fool her. She knows
my kind—the ones who build fences, shoot her sisters.

But as I work to pull the wires apart, she drops
to her knees—waiting, perhaps hoping. Once
I catch my fingers between the wires, panic
when they won't release me. My pain must be
sharp as her fear, but I'm not the one bleeding.

When I release myself I huff and puff
up the hill to borrow wire clippers.
Find my friend who drives us back to the deer.
All the while we hope she's broken loose,
but, of course, she hasn't.

The clippers are meant for lighter wire,
but we take turns cutting, twisting, pulling—
surprised when the wire lets go.

The deer limps to a copse of trees,
and we wince to see her white bone.

The firs shiver in the wind, silent witnesses like us,
praying she'll make it, knowing she probably won't.
It's cold. She's in shock. Come darkness, coyotes
will hunt her. All night my pinkie finger throbs—the scarlet
welt round as a tiny hoof, tattoo of another creature's terror.

Spring Poem

Dark universe: is *fire*
    part of the weather? They say
That when the permafrost melts,
    the climate will be
"Unrecognizable." So let's say the systematic
    change comes to pass, which seems
Unlikely: wouldn't *that*
    curtail our lives in exactly
The ways we refuse
    to curtail them, ourselves? Or are we hoping
That within the systematic there's a trap
    door to conferences in Europe? Today outside
It's green, periwinkle, and brown. There
    are *bits* of purple in the lawn, those dainty
Four-inch high bright stars
    my older women friends all know
The name of. Past them (the flowers, that is) I saw my cat
    chase a squirrel nearly her size. She didn't hear
The guy on the radio last night say kids these days
    are dual citizens of two worlds, the digital
And the regular. He said it as though both
    are equally autonomous and real. Epistemologically,
Sure. But ontologically? I'm pretty sure the internet
    can't exist without the earth. At least,
I can't. Nor can James Schuyler, writing
    about roses, how much he loves them, writing
In his undershorts. Half the time he didn't know
    the names of flowers, either. I learned one

This week, that of the primrose outside
    my front door, a flat-faced violet beauty. Its color deep
And thick like felted wool, not airy like those others
    in the lawn, which come to think of it are squills. And come
To think of it some more, they're not at all purple but the freaky,
    translucent blue of polar ice. I'd really love
For everyone to face up to the inverse
    relationship between flowers and flying. This whole
Poem is a poem against dirtying up the earth,
    because I wrote none of it buying. I'm trying
To make it almost entirely powered
    by the sun. I wouldn't want to see cartoony pictures
Of fire in the weather report, would you?
    No, not a single one.

To Father

I can still smell creosote,
hear stones crunch underfoot,
see the sun reflecting on the thin,
glowing bars of steel.

A boy in a coal town,
you watched the trains,
processions of coal cars—
black and black
and black and black—
that crossed the railroad bridge
over the muddy Susquehanna River
in Nanticoke, Pennsylvania,
water thick and brown as chocolate milk
after heavy summer rains.

In your dreams, those trains carried you
out of that coal town, to places less black,
where, years later, you would live—
Paris, Stuttgart, Brussels, and the suburbs
of Philadelphia and Washington, D.C.,
where the lawns were large and green,
and even the sun seemed brighter.

But the black stayed with you.
You remembered the piles of culm by the roadside—
like dirty snow that never melted.
So, you always went back, as if paying a debt,
to that town surrounded by coal mines

and filled with hard-working people like your father—
many of them German, Polish, and Welsh immigrants,
who worked at night during the day
down in the black mines,
burrowing through the damp earth like moles,
emerging black-faced and white-eyed
to greet wives wearing floral print dresses,
who kissed their husbands goodbye
for the last time every morning.
Their children would grow
to see the mines close,
and the town grow poor.

Now I walk alone,
where you once walked with me,
but the tracks are abandoned
and overgrown with grass
like a forgotten grave.

Antonio Vallone

Pack Horse Librarians

for Carrie Bishop, my favorite librarian

If you lived
during the Great Depression,
you might have seen
or heard about,
at least,
women on horseback,

some, from a distance,
who looked like men
dressed in canvas
work pants and Stetsons,
some in the weekday cotton dresses
they'd normally wear to work,
riding astride
on muddy trails
that followed creek banks
in the hollers of Kentucky.

They carted books
in saddle bags
and brought news
from far beyond

the forested hills
to the people who lived
in these hardscrabble nooks
and coal towns.

They left the safety
of their clean and quiet
shelf-lined rooms,
shining the light
of words
into mine-like darkness,
beginning to map out
a means of escape.

The World Populated with Ghosts

First, your grandfather leaves
his body behind
and sometime later your grandmother.

Then, a kid in your high school
you didn't like that much anyway
is found by his father
dead in the woods
while deer hunting,
sitting as if taking a nap,
back against a tree,
slumped over, still
holding his rifle,
and another you sat with
in the cafeteria some days during lunch
shot himself in the vice principal's office.

Your parents come back
into your lives, this time as patients
you help care for,
then they disappear, leaving you
orphaned.

      One by one,
your friends die
as well as the great writers and artists
you looked up to in your youth.

Eventually, you're left alone
with a table and chairs, paper,
fountain pens and ink,

ghosts sitting in the empty seats,
nodding or bobbing their heads
to music you can't hear,
drumming their ghostly fingers
on the table top,
stealing glances at their watches,
hoping you won't see.

The Scullery Maid

Victim # 243: Unknown

Morgue entry: *Female age 35 to 40. Fair complexion. Large nose. Tall and strangely built . . . Working woman, Hands creased—evidently worked about a stove . . .*

In between basting and boiling, scouring and mopping, I'd lean
against the back-porch rail of the St. Charles Hotel and gaze
up to the hills.

When sails appeared like seraphim on the mountain lake, gliding
against the dark pine ridge, I let myself be lifted into that vision;

imagined myself as one of those fancy Club House ladies with
starched petticoats, a smart bonnet trimmed with bows and flowers,
a wide silk ribbon tied 'neath my chin.

My hands would be smooth as the marble Virgin's at St John's;
not these rough, puckered mitts that know only serve and scrub
day in and out.

I'd be handed into a boat fitted with wings, white wings, stretched out
like a sea bird's, and float right off the mountain.

Oh such fantasies! Until old Mr. Fitzharris hollers, on the regular,
to get back to the kitchen.

By 11:00 that morning, water in the streets already head-high; no time
to take up the rugs—I was swept up the stairs with all creation, jamming
and shouting, *Run for your life! The dam failed!* when the wave crashed

with such a force it dragged me back down; all the way down to the cellar where they discovered me, days later, floating among jars of peaches and beans. My cotton underskirt flared about my body.

The Drifter

Victim # 64: Unknown

> Morgue entry: *Male. 30 years . . . Open faced silver watch. 1 knife.*
> *1 rule. 1 toothbrush. 1 lead pencil. Book of rates E.L.A.S.*
> *1000 miles pass book.*

Here's the design: hop the Pennsylvania line
at East Conemaugh then on upstate to the Erie-New
York, all the way into St. Louis, change to the Frisco.
West, where the outlook opens wide: blue skies, sea-
washed air.

Yes sir, the Iron Horse, my way out of this smoke-
choked town. Sick to death of my skin crawling
with dust; crunching soot in my sleep.

Anyways, no job, no family; nothin' here
to root me. I'm carrying everything a fella needs
to strike out—my father's silver time piece,
valuable as my 1,000-mile pass—good as gold
in my pocket.

A knife, of course. What man worth his salt doesn't
carry some sort of blade? A rule, a pencil, a book of
rates. How many hot meals, tobacco plugs, shoe
shines, miles. Got it figured. Exacting, down to the
eighth inch, the last copper—that's me.

Rain still lashing this morning like a coachwhip.
A dark mist arcing over the hill, like some fine black

powder spewing straight out the ground. Best high-tail it
toward the station.

What now! That ear-splitting thunder,
some fearsome rumble
booming down the mountainside?

The Carpenter

Victim # 84: Unknown

Morgue entry: *Male. Age 45. Height 6 ft. Very powerful man.*
Sandy hair . . . Bullet head. Massive jaws. On his right
arm was tattooed a ballet dancer with a tambourine
in her hand. Knees calloused as though he worked
at measuring. Expression indicated Irish nativity.

My life was hoist, measure, pound. Making houses sturdy as myself, houses for the big bugs along Washington Street the jewelers and bankers. Nothing but the best for that breed: braced framing, concrete slab, walls plumb as plumb is plumb.

So much a body reveals: my roughed-up knees read *measure*, feet bare and pocked announced hobnail shoes. Those shoes swallowed up by the flux and filth. My jaw, square as a four-walled room. Beale figured it right—my hands were indeed a fighter's. Any man, hey, I could thump him flat as a thick-shank nail.

But this torrent! A roil of saw logs, brick, axles, cattle and swine. Christ-a-mighty! The whole hillside come down upon us like all wrath. They found me wedged in a stone foundation of a house I set right. For all my mass, I was no match for that water's brawn, its gnarled fist.

Hornet Nest

My college-aged son and I are
two bucks. Our chests touching, we
catch our horns on chandeliers, in coat hangers.
When I'm home, he stays clear of my grazing area.
When I'm gone, he becomes me. When we talk, my
temples sting. Once, on the Appalachian Trail, we agreed.
He was ten. We hiked a lot then—with rock hammers. We
picked up quartz or granite from the trail, chipped it, put
samples in our knapsacks. Keeping up meant following
him across boulders, into caves, to side paths, always
behind, hearing—never seeing—frogs plopping
into ponds, startled turkeys flapping for takeoff,
the thrash of leaves as foxes ran, the shrieks of
pileated woodpeckers. That one time, he had
stopped to wait near a tree-hung hornet nest.
Big as an urn, it was a perfect target. Though
stung by conscience, I seized a chunk of
quartz, threw it, but missed wide. My son,
the accomplice, chipped granite into
throwable pieces. The hornets, at
every hit, clouded the sky. We
kept it up, my son seeing,
at last, his father. The
hornets, unimpressed,
swore: "Once you
lock on, sting
the hell out
of them."

Wisdom of Shadows

i.
You are wise, Grandmother, in the knowing
of the sheep sorrel
and timothy grass, the tearthumb
and agrimony,
growing in the harrowed field
by your burrow
where you hibernate
until the young shoots sprout.

To know the right time is to know everything.

ii.
Seven wolves caught a groundhog. "Now we will kill you," they said,
"for something to eat." The Wise One responded, "Such a wonderful
    occasion
calls for a Dance! I will whistle a song for you. Let us use these seven
    trees that grow
in a circle, and dance among them. At the last tree, you can kill me."

The wolves rose up on their hind legs and danced from tree to tree
behind the whistle-pig, in the dappled shade, on the soft mossy
    ground.
"Such fine dancing!" the Wise One said.

Each dance became longer than the last.

At the seventh tree, the Wise One said, "Go ahead of me, you fine
dancers, so I can enjoy your skill as I whistle this last song. Then, you
can kill me."

At the final sweet note, the wolves turned. The Wise One dove into her burrow at the root of the seventh tree. The tip of her tail was caught by the quickest wolf and broke off. Her tail has been short ever since.**

Sometimes the wisest thing is to let go.

iii.
Groundhog, Woodchuck, Wood-shock,
Thickwood Badger,
Chuck.
Wojak, Weenusk, Whistle-pig,
Ground-pig.
Red
Monk.
Marmot monax,
Moonack.
Ground squirrel,
Digger.

The wise go by many names and are therefore nameless.

iv.
The animals know more than we know.
The robin sees the predator
we don't see, the dog hears
the footstep we don't hear.
The cow knows rain is coming
and lies down,
the wooly caterpillar
tells of time to come,
the woodchuck emerges to predict
the future in the light.

There is wisdom in the shadows.

The Loom

unstrung, blonde frame wide,
shimmering heddles loose,
the reed in repose,
the pedals slack—

as I shuttle to meetings,
race to destinations;
the warp of my time
threaded with expectations,
the weft, obligations;
    and endings loom ahead.

Everyday Things

My dog wakes me
in the dark morning
with a whine
so I slip from my bed,
out the door—
the half-moon cast in mist,
forest quieted by fog
the last clinging leaves damp.

She lifts her head to sniff;
my eyes take in shrouds
of suspended moonlight—

everyday things
emerge wondrous.

Long-fingered hemlocks,
hardwoods with faint stars entangled,
    the dry stalks of the grasses,
and where she looks
I hear the barest
beckoning whisper.

Afrolachia

I went west to Appalachia
like a finger tracing a line from the Qur'an.

The whiteness covered the hills
like clean sheets falling on blistered skin.

I went east to West Africa
like a Césairian run-on sentence.

The blackness poured rivers
like licorice melting in a Moroccan bathhouse.

The faces: white with black beards,
black with white beards.

The faces: all torn through and weathered,
all dried-up river and ripped-up mountain.

The forest swallows the yardstick and coughs up coal;
the desert burns the meterstick and pukes out people.

Appalachia|Africa: all lines drawn from foreign verses—
I hear the elders' voices crack.

Lunch at the Korner Restaurant

It is the kind of place
where men dip their fries in mayo
and debate the wisdom of swapping out a
universal joint while using an adaptor kit.

"The garage is so busy, my dog is answering the phone.
Charlie—-how you been? No one sees your face anymore."
"Alright, I guess, except I'm stiff where I used to be limber
and limber where I used to be stiff."

Two 30-something men from the machine shop across the street
stop in for rhubarb pie and ice cream.
"Listen, if you can't fix it, you gotta learn to stand it."
"I know, I know, but I don't want to lose her."

In the rear booth, a deep sigh is
followed by a cigarette–honed voice:
"Backhoes and laptops have been my whole morning.
What neck-tied engineer dreamed that one up?"

"The Stillers need to cut loose from Big Ben. He's done.
Past his prime, 300 lbs, bad elbow, pouts too much."
"Hey, you're confusing him with Bradshaw."
"No, Ben has better hair."

I sit here listening with nowhere to join in.
Universal joint repair? I know nothing.
What about universal health care, or the universe?
How did it begin? How will it end?

Relationship break-up? I've had a few, but
am no authority for advice-giving.
What about discussing fate versus free will?
How can we lose what we don't possess?

I could comment on the perils of aging,
the frustration of uncooperative laptops,
the Steelers, Pens, and Pirates.
But, I don't. I just ask for the check.

Another Hike

Another hike, another boundless view,
another something else beyond the hill,
or maybe it's the Alps I should pursue,
the sharper, farther peak could give a thrill.
And then what? And then where? Won't I aim higher?
Is a Himalayan trek the next quest?
Will whatever prompts this urgent desire,
end when I reach the top of Everest?
Why can't this rocky hilltop crag suffice,
and that valley, those woods, the river bridge,
the clustered settlement—to be precise
that third house by the church with the crossed ridge?
In truth it does, and here's why: the way down,
the stumbling, aching footsteps back to town.

Nippenose Valley

The story of place is a crooked story
The story of a family is worse
   —Jane Mead

Our father's people are from a place
where men come at life hard
and women dig at their nail beds.
We're in the woods, my brother and I,
behind the old house aiming at a milk jug
weighted with dirt, dead leaves, and orange juice gone bad.

It's a damp, yet crisp morning,
the ground is soft and slick, the fog lifted,
the air riddles with smoke from a neighboring farm's burn pile.
In November the fields look shamed by their nakedness,
the woods too—
naked, but for hunters' orange camo.

I pull back the hammer of a .357
(as heavy as it looks) hit the jug with the first shot.
We carry the bodies of those country rough men
and the bodies of their uprooted children and trees.
As a kid I thought I was tough shit,
but I couldn't hold the power of a .54 percussion rifle.
The double-barrel slammed my lip, almost split it through.
My father rubbed dirt in my mouth to stop the bleeding,
said I was lucky I didn't break my nose.

We carry the sound of cold autumn days
being cracked open with a single blast.
Off these back roads everyone has guns,
some keep pistols in bedside tables
for when the night is broken.

Only two things a man should feel—sarcasm and anger,
the rest (sadness/old photos/tenderness/a child's lock of hair/whiskey/
    love)
he buries in his gut hoping it won't twist into a cancer.

We go through half a carton of bullets.
The sun just about set, my brother carries the revolver
wearing Dad's old holster. I carry the empty shells
back to the house,
the air is hollow and heavy,
we leave the riddled jug behind.

Coal Towns of Pennsylvania

By their names do we know them,
and what they were about:

Nanty Glo, to start,
Welsh for
"where the coal is."

Carbon, and Carbondale.

Ashland, with its Mothers Statue
and the Connellsville Coal Field,

where the local cops shot
ten striking miners dead.

Oh, how the rage burned
deep in those dark holes, and
secret meetings!

Where it erupted, blood flowed
and the towns gave their names to
the local slaughter:

The Morewood Massacre:
six brothers dead.
In Lattimer, nineteen
and Windber, three more.
Westmoreland: six killed
(plus nine miners' wives.)

But sometimes,
names were just names,
or names from names:
Imperial, named for the coal company.
Gilberton, named for the mine owner
and Mary D, for the owner's wife.

Or towns named
for the mine itself:

Number Thirty Seven
Oliphant Furnace
Reading Number Three

In Centralia, deep underground,
the mine still burns.

When Two Bodies

Bob says I'm beautiful so I like him.
Also, he brings me zucchini.
Bob is losing his memory. He came to the party
two hours early. He helped me,
and we talked about 1962 East Berlin.

They had never seen an American uniform —no,
maybe they had and thought I was a ghost.

Bob needs help out of the chair. When I grab hold
of his shoulders, he makes the sign of the cross.
His dandelion beard feathers my cheek. He forgets
who I am but he can tell I'm *a-okay.*
Bob wishes me a good 50th year. He says,

I don't care that you cut through my yard
to go to Carol's. I like seeing young people.

How better to move through this mess
of houses? How better to know each other?
At the BBQ, someone dismisses Bob
as a drunk, as if crying isn't justified
when two bodies lift each other up.

River Child

My first river flowed north,
ran little eddies by the high school,
carried coal dust up to New York.

When I go home now,
I leave three rivers in the rearview.
Cross the Allegheny, the Conemaugh,
Susquehanna, and Pine Creek, until
the highway carries me to the Tioga River.

I race it to Gramma's Kitchen, the university,
to Mansfield, the mountains, to the county
that carries that river's name. Tioga means
the place where the river forks.
I have always been of this divided flow.

In elementary school, they told us
that the Nile also flowed north.
We thought these rivers were the only ones
who could overcome gravity, that we
were second only to the Nile.

When we were that young, the Tioga was orange.
That didn't stop us from getting into it,
dyeing our white Walmart sneakers with the pollution,
slipping and splitting our knees on the rocks.

Mountain Avenue Sylvania

There is still Armenia Mountain
dirt, red and warm, in the lines
of my feet, lacing my toenails,
caking my heels.

I missed the mountain
before I even wound down it,
before I locked the cabin door
with the key on the inside,
before I stifled the final embers
of last night's fire.

When I'm on the mountain, I don't
have to think about the men in town
who've had their hands on me,
the cousins who keep an eye out,
the father who has his buddies tail my car.

Every time I decide to go back,
I remember that there are more people
I can't contend with than places hiring,
more opioid arrests than students
in my graduating class.

Now, at the mouth of Mountain Avenue,
my brakes grind as I hover in second gear
thinking of yesterday. Cased in cold spring water,
each breath slicing through me,
I stared at the ring of trees above.

Upon Hearing Brooklyn Street will be Paved

Defying development, Brooklyn Street
snakes along the banks of the northward Tioga,
creeping behind houses, farms, a beauty shop.
It has carried me undetected, kept watchful
townies from finding me on my way
to get high at Mill Cove, buy condoms at Walmart,
or head onto Route 15 before my father wakes.

The town has already built a Verizon store,
a Dollar Tree by the Dunkin',
a second and then a third stoplight.
Brooklyn Street connects them all,
running from one side of town to the other.

I have to go slow on Brooklyn Street,
maneuver each curve like I haven't
taken it before, like I didn't
come home to that street when I was born.

The year they put in the Sheetz,
someone overdosed in the apartment
above the bookstore I worked at in high school,
a man shot his wife on Route 6
after she tried to leave him,
and a girl died on Brooklyn Street.

She totaled her car going 65,
not knowing that the red gravel
warrants no more than a careful 30.
I still haven't seen a cross for her.

I hope Brooklyn Street is never paved.
I hope it spews dust forever,
stays crooked and dangerous
like all the girls who need it.

Migration

What do these red-winged blackbirds know
of the man who killed himself,

what do they know in their abundance
from here in Pennsylvania's cattails

of the Honduran migrant whose name we've not
been told, who was crowded into one of those

Texas family detention centers? I'm listening
to the female birds' scolding

chatter; I'm listening for the world's
rotation into grief. Experts say

this will not be the last death. At dusk,
the flock fills an anonymous tree.

Germination, 2020

First day of spring, gray air,
gray road, brown flowered cattails in the ditch begin

their slow explosion
while we stand and watch the seeded

fluff rise on the breeze.
Coltsfoot is the first

to flower here in the waste
between gravel and field,

yellow buttons
the size of dimes,

brought from Europe
and Asia as medicine, and so

named *Tussilago* from the Latin
tussin for "cough" and *ago*

for "act upon."
Its stem

and leaves are formed like the fetlocked leg
of the horse in the distant neighbor's

pasture during these quiet days
of fever and fear.

The Ohio Again Nightbird of Memory

What hypochondriacal woman probably dies tonight
On the seventh floor wrapped in the concupiscence of
Antiseptic and cottons dryer-radiant? She has never
Let go like this before, beholds her body near the wall
Before the curtain, a library of Steubenvillian vowels.
The clippity-clop shuffle of the night nurse who marks
Something small in his book, and his *uh-huh* muttering
Might be the muttering of her body as it sharpens
Every character into crocodile. And when he pivots,
Attending to his rounds, she cuts for the water's edge.
She is attending to hers, comes to remember the river
Corrugated and varicose as a dimpled thigh.

Step down betwixt the waterfowl, learn where the lights
From Wheeling trawl among the black wakes of barges.

Moundsville Nocturne

these are the ones
left behind

who prowl these parts
like panthers

roaming alone
sometimes in packs

they leave their prints in ash
under bridges, in vacant factories,

slender cigarettes,
with no filters

sometimes, you catch a glimpse
of one, a snarl of smoke,

a lean shadow beneath a streetlight,
his eyes glow yellow in the dark

that's how you know
there's something in there

that's how you know
he's still alive

ready to pounce

Crossing State Lines, Again

Sometimes they walk
from West Virginia to Ohio
just looking for something to do

Sometimes they get dolled up
to watch the barges haul coal
from a different angle
or to use their food stamps
at a new gas station

Sometimes they hitch a ride
with guys who buy them beer
and take them to the kinds of places

they can't get to by walking—
apartment complexes,
coal chutes, train bridges,

and sometimes one of them stays
all night on the Ohio side
and one of them runs home
runs home, all the way home

Little Charlie on the River

What we need 'round here is riverboat gambling.
Can't you see me working on a riverboat?
Hell, I'll start me my own,
call it the *Little Charlie*.
I'd have to take out a loan to get it,
but I'd make my money back
in about four or five weeks.
You see, I know how to fix a deck.
The trick's in the wrist.
Here, move your hand like this.
Ain't too bad.
I suppose I could teach you,
get you a job on the *Little Charlie*.
It's the free drinks and the beautiful women,
we're talking high class ladies,
not like them girls down there at the Wet 'n' Wild.
You see that coal barge over there?
I used to throw rocks at them when I was little,
Couldn't hit 'em back then.
I could now but I'm too tired to try.
Got locked up last night. DUI.
I thought about moving out to Vegas
but they ain't got the Ohio River out there.

Kansas Barbed Wire Museum

. . . they dug a hole, placed all their anger in it,
and agreed to live peacefully
      —Lodge of Tales

Crandal's Champion, 1879; Buckthorn, 1881; Twisted Oval, 1881
    On the lands of the Sioux Tribal Headquarters, you can eat
    buffalo
    burgers at Medro's Tee-Pee Restaurant. The moccasins sold
    there read Made in Korea.

Glidden Railroad Wire, 1872; Big Buffalo, 1876; Spurrowed, 1887
    On the lands of the Crow Reservation, clapboard houses peel
    and lean
    toward Appalachia. The AFL-CIO Paycheck Temple features
    happy hour
    from 4-7 p.m. daily.

Necktie, 1878; Sawtooth Ribbon, 1881; Decker's Spread, 1884
    The roads on this land shoulder horse grass and hairy vetch. A
    call to the Harvest
    Pow-wow takes a truck drive past Crazy Woman Creek. Lodge
    poles and folded
    skins hum down the four-lane with indecent orange plastic
    strips flying to keep me from
    following too closely.

Seven Strand, 1876; Clinchwire, 1876; Scutt's Clip, 1885
    At Smash-in-Head-Buffalo-Jump, the Blood Tribe used a secret
    better than horses.

Over the cliff, a spill of buffalo into a blanket of bones. The
    herds fed the tribes.
The buffalo horns fed munitions production.

As generation upon generation fell, the tribes grew hungrier and
hungrier.

Other Than That

I have heard/That guilty creatures sitting at a play/Have, by the very cunning of the scene,/Been struck so to the soul that presently/They have proclaimed their malefactions.
  —Hamlet, II.ii.

How many men and women
are sitting on front porches
around the country right now,
jugs of limeade asweat at their
elbows, tobacco smoke
in the air, conversations
about Johnny Rotten or Chuck
Taylor or Kiyoshi Kurosawa
still redolent with the taste
of barbecued cauliflower served
on a crosshatched bed of asparagus?
And how many more sit behind
the bars on the windows
of the psych wards, sit at long white
institutional formica tables, poke
at bland mashed potatoes
and beige gravy, listen to the rain
and remember how it tastes,
the everpresent sound of TV news
from behind like the chitter
of cicadas whose taste they have
also almost forgotten? How much
time is there before the guy
with more guitar than talent pulls

it out, tries to involve everyone
in a singalong of "Feelings"
or "Sweet Caroline" or "American
Idiot"? Did anyone leave the oven on?
Did anyone bring the mayo, the pho,
the seven decks of cards necessary
to play your grandmother's version
of euchre? Are we ready for our
close-ups? And who's the DP on this
project anyway? Have we determined
the proper ratio of sugar to lime zest,
patients to therapists, Morris Albert
to Neil Diamond? The sun sinks.

Objects in Mirror

Life is love and love is loss and loss is the Ohio horizon.
Growth is the learning of maps, and fate is a braided road:
Route 13 intertwined with Sunday Creek
and the Norfolk Southern rails.

Memory is a valley and history, lips that whisper
in the weight of a summer thunder noon.

I slow for the curve that drops me into Moxahala.
The name sparks my brow like a half-forgotten incantation,
a secret lock of sounds lost to time.

Once this place was its own universe, that word the world to one
who staked a claim to a name, and hoped to frame it forever.
Today, it's a roadside sign, an empty spell.

I want to fill my lungs with one last song for Moxahala, the song that
    danced
on the lips of whoever first spoke the name and called it home.

And as I watch Moxahala fall through my fingers
on the rear-view mirror, I will not think
it stands for anything else.

This is not about you.
This is not about you.

Self-quarantine

Contiguous to the room's plane of light
is your lined face stamped with Suffering,
the aches of age and diminishment turning on
like lightning-stitchings branched to blue earth.
You're saying how unfair it is, the way women
age one way and men another. I agree, but then
change the subject and say I plucked a dollar-bill
from the street after a storm once, unmistakable

paper swept on by runoff. If it has a soundtrack,
luck, I offer that it kicks off with the Pink Floyd song
"Money," Fortune's ringtone. And just when I imagine
the flash mislaid, the developing thunder has its say.
You're pouting. It's a pretty pout, but the pandemic
could care less if anyone lives, dies. I don't say that.
We're going to be inside together for some time, as
we're at risk for a bug which is stilling American life,

industry. And the streets of Rome: the Pope has just
cancelled Easter services as if resurrection only gets
you so far. I don't know what to say. I tell you I had
this dog who "slew" (and I use the word) an Eastern
gray squirrel. *She ran it down*, I say, *in roaring greed.*
Even though we're old, both of us, this may lead to sex.
Or the closeness we keep letting replace that Something
healed us in those days before all this talk of quarantines.

Either you understand these are always matters of life and
death, or I've misjudged you. Still, I don't say I saw light
leave those black eyes. Irreplaceable life-once-only eyes.
Or that the lens closest to me took a selfie of my mouth
opening and closing like the doors to the Hall of Luck,
saying how sorry I was as blood streamed and fell,
landing as wide drops from the rheumy gray ribs
and the place in the fur opened like torn bread.

C. Dubielak

After Yan Sun's Red Ribbon

I'm waiting on some lo mein in the only Chinese
restaurant in my county—one more than we have Walmarts,
one less than millionaire farmers. The same as we have
coal mines, just the one now, the weighted train
with its load weaving the ribbon of track
northeast, then northwest, like a drunken ghost
as we sleep. In Cheng's, two little girls,
finished with their schoolwork, sit in their booth
while their father tosses Chinese cabbage
in hot woks and their mother ends every phone call
with "twenty minutes." There isn't much
to do but people-watch, and they are
watching me as I put a quarter in an old vending
machine. This promises to be something worth watching.
The older sister shimmies to the end of her seat
while I extract the prize from its plastic bubble. It's a ring.
A gaudy one, to be sure, bright pink, perfect
for her demographic. "Beautiful," she says.
I find two more quarters in my bag, say "one for you
and one for your sister." They crank the machine
and run to the counter to show their mother the prize.
My lo mein is ready; she thanks me when I pay,
and I thank her, too. We are not natives here, but we are
mothers, far from family except our own. My mother
has never understood why I live where there's nothing
compared to the city where I was raised. How
do I explain it? It's tree shade in summer, and
wood smoke in winter. Wild black raspberries and my sons
who learned to eat them off the vine. It's no traffic

or noise except that train as it grinds through
the deep curve behind my woods. Even that will
eventually come to an end. Long after coal
is no longer worth digging, berries will grow,
children will pick them, and my bones
will be here at rest.

Fall Colors

An oil drum melts
in the river, tentacles of rust
flailing in the current.

Tendrils finger water
sliding beneath grapevines
grown to a leaning willow.

Thin fish swim
through shotgun holes,
dark algae clogs their gills.

Dusky grapes
fall and burst
on the river bank,

a few bruises, an open wound.

Charitable Donations

The grizzled men selling
paper roses at crosswalks
know the time of day.
Judicious tongues harangue
spit-polished passersby
on the evils of wealth,
while the ping of every coin
in a tin cup adds up
to another round of sin.
It is too easy to say
that the bridges linking
Ohio and West Virginia
lead from one man's hell
to another man's heaven,
and that the gambling boats
floating below make up
Purgatory's fleet. Nevertheless,
many fathers have taken
that long first step off the side
and not come up again until
it's too late for a breath of air.

La Brea

In a Los Angeles park, dark bones of animals surface,
preserved in tar for 38,000 years. Here, in Ohio,
coal mine fires were intentionally set and have burned
beneath the earth for 130 years. Nearby, well water

is warm enough to brew tea, but who would drink it?
In the smoldering blackness, 82 miners buried
in the Millfield cave-in whisper stories of methane leaks
to men under the Upper Big Branch slag pile

whose bodies may never surface. You can walk the woods
and see dusty smoke drift out from the damp hillside.
Does the timber rattler nest in the warmed mine shafts?
Now injection wells and evaporation stations line these roads

like altars to extinction, gas flares of gold shimmer in the dusk.
Layers of clouds stand apart from the sky but are still sky.
We have heard that oil and water do not mix,
yet here, we see that they might do that.

This fire, this dark heat, like blood behind our breath,
it seeps into us, we hug our pets closer
while coyotes scream, but still we keen to that shrill sound.
How can we know what is not yet imagined?

How does it feel to take despair by the hand
and gaze into its dark heart? Will anyone want this place

when there is no longer anything to extract?
Once in dense fog, I could not see the earth

beneath my feet, once I heard crows scream
on a misty horizon, once I stood in a rainstorm beside a lake
while the shoreline boiled over into sky.
Never mind how the sun broke the haze. Instead,

there is this forsaken purpose, this pint jar of tar,
this dark brush, like time, seeping through,
and these uneasy bones, stained with age,
they wait their turns to rise.

Thanksgiving at the Soup Opera

I can't remember when I first learned to eat, but I remember
taking my babies off the breast and hoping
they got enough nourishment from mashed peas and sweet potatoes
that they crammed between their smacking lips.

Say "Aaah," I'd say, spoon by spoon, opening my mouth too,
I wanted them to trust, to know that someone
would provide. "More," they'd say when they were old enough to talk,
and "mine" when they didn't want to share,

grinding food between gums. I am reminded of this
at the Soup Opera when I see the folks who choose soup
to dip day-old bread and soften crusts. Where else can they go
but here? Outside an ambulance screams, waiting for drivers

to clear the road. This is Fairmont Avenue, downtown Fairmont,
West Virginia. No one lives in the mansion on the hill.
We all wake to the six a.m. mine report. *Farmington won't work,*
Martinka won't work. We all watch the sun sink

earlier each day. Icicles hang like spikes from gables
between buildings, doorways are nailed over in plywood,
windows are blank with brick. Today, like yesterday, I talk to Sue
about how our boys are grown and gone, how the town's soul

seems to have slipped through the shaky hands
that line up here. Her farmhouse caved in from mine subsidence,
she can't stand the air in the new trailer, the bottled water.
Don't seem right. We keep an eye out for Betty,

her white shock of hair and thick hands, there was that vague way
the newspaper announced her son's death, we are almost glad
that her husband went first. Jim used to roll his oxygen tank
through the door, hold her coat and her purse, pull out a chair

for Betty to settle into. Church bells strike noon, more folks
fill long tables to eat donated food, some murmur, some sigh,
some hold babies or small children while I cut onions, potatoes,
open cans of stock, give thanks for the smells and the noises

of the kitchen. Fake candles flicker on the tables.
We keep the food warm and the lights low in this place of soup
and gratitude, we catch the sudden shimmer
of the sun in the broken glass on the curb. We hope

that things can be made better one onion at a time,
we hold on hard to memories, these faces in the rearview mirror,
like my boys in the backseat, sweet and shining
as always.

This rocky soil

Out of spite, I break morning
with the sky a canopy of icy blue.

Swords of sunlight crackle the surface
of the pond, and the eagle's huge nest

stands empty at the top of the sycamore.
There is more to finding

than what we set out to look for.
There are graves here,

they keep me company, faithful
like hounds, when they know.

There are horses, chewing,
heavy horses that always seem

to need food, and six buzzards,
circling the valley in rounds of sorrows,

divided by high ridges of mist. This texture
of life, it does not protect us

from dreams of terror. A deer
sheds its antlers, small creatures

pick the bones bare, whatever remains
some smaller insect will scratch

from this almost frozen ground.
Things that remain unbroken

still get scars. In the sky,
the slimmest shadow of a moon,

sky, then moon, then sky again,
and though each step I take

may reveal nothing
to those who come after me,

I will take this rocky soil
and try to dig.

Stephanie Kendrick

Rural America Gets a Visitor During the Coronavirus

The heads of whatever departments are telling us
that the National Guard is coming,
this time without guns,
armed with loaves of bread
and boxes of whatever food might ease
the hunger, and what I would like
to let them know is that this is not enough,
that we are a people familiar with starvation, tired
of heroes handing us things
we are not desperate for, and where
will the men in uniform go when we can leave
our homes, and those of us who give
daily are no longer televised,
will they come again
to put our ground back underneath our soil, to
soak the acid from our water and drain distrust
from our parents' chests?

We Don't Own Shit, Ya Know

This is what I tell my son when he says loud
that I oughta kill a snake after it dances
on my toes in low grass as I rid my yard
of the sticks that look just like it. Well hell
yes I am afraid & I threw those damn sticks
down so fast & did my own little dance
I know my neighbors laughed & I fixed
my eyes on that momma
(you can tell by the tail) racer & dared
to blink. We don't own the grass
that we must mow, lest a fine be taped large
on our front door & I still smash the blades
with bare soles & get pissy when they stain
my heels & we are not the kings nor queens
(you can tell by the tale) of the trees
we pick from & pick at & pick apart, no
we don't get to decide the life of a seed.
Women know this, as we have tried
and failed so many times,
Gods to our cores.
We need these snakes,
I say & if we rid the world
of venom & fang, how would we know
the difference between a kiss and a bite.

Perfect Pitch

I rode middle school-bound
in the back seat of my aunt's station wagon,
listening to her and mamma sing "Jolene,"
trading verses, harmonizing the chorus,
I'm begging of you please don't take my man!

A few years later it was "9 to 5."
They were fired up and it was Dolly's doing.
This was rural Ohio, the bottom lip
of Northern Appalachia,
right shy of Perry Como country.

The women in my family worked
the TS Trim factory, spitting out
Honda car parts. Started out
on the assembly line, worked their way
up to paint, then detailing, then welding.

The physical labor made their bodies strong,
their future bright and like Dolly,
they weren't taking any shit.
They learned early on about strikes and picket lines,
how important it was to organize and vote.

Brave women in the work force determined
to see their daughters inside college classrooms,
the hell out of factory row.
I didn't know then that I was being raised
by a feminist, taking back her power.

Like Dolly, my mamma would never use that word,
no matter how much she embodied it.
She was proud to hang up her welder's helmet
end of shift, pick up her paycheck, sing in the front seat
of a station wagon with women she loved.

Elemental

Sand melts into glass all colors of the moon.
The moon gazes back with crater eyes
as tides lift bottles of lost hopes crashing
against boulders from which they came.
And in these hills, every rock cliff and holler
cups secrets and time.

There is nothing new under the sun.
What we toss aside comes back again,
or works its way downriver to land
on someone else's shore, yet there's
comfort in knowing we don't
need to reinvent the world.

Seasons cycle on, atoms rearrange.
We gather around a fire, listen to waves
of wind sluice through corn stalks, stare up
at ancient stars whose old light still delights.
The house, once green wood, bears scars,
worm trails twisting unreadable scripts.

Our lives are glass—amorphous solids,
never just one thing—
always another evolving.

We rise up, break down, become—
spinning brief beautiful tales
out of dust.

David B. Prather

Treatment at Fairmont General

Wayne is the name I gave that guy on the psych ward
    who hanged himself

with twisted sheets from the corner of a bed.
    The staff rushed him

past my room one afternoon while I looked out the window
    at what little I could see

of Fairmont, West Virginia. I called him Wayne
    because he reminded me

of someone I went to school with, and because
    the drugs made me not care

about remembering. Which I do now. He told me
    his wife left him,

wouldn't let him see his son or his daughter.
    I told him none of my secrets.

I knew he wouldn't listen. There was a touch of snow
    and a hint of sunlight.

There was a pine tree shivering. There was traffic
    below. I don't know

what became of my classmate whose name I gave
    away. All I remember is

he loved horses and corny jokes. But that's something,
    isn't it?

That's something to keep you alive.

David B. Prather

The Plight of Frankenstein's Monster

How it was done, I can't say,
the top of the head cut loose,
the brain of someone forgotten

attached and articulated
with each sensitive nerve.
Is it any wonder

I've always felt out of place?
Perhaps I suffer a medical
disorder or a crisis of identity,

my inner self incompatible
with my outward appearance.
Who is it? Who stitched

these fingertips into their whorls
and loops? I don't know how,
but someone picked up every bone

and glued them together with flayed
portions of muscle. The organs
keep shifting, unsure in their places,

afraid of rejection.
My sex is foreign, my skin a patchwork
of cells and dust. What is the thread

that holds me together?
Will these wounds ever heal?
Are there any balms or tinctures,

any ointments or salves to soothe
my frayed edges? All these parts,
I can only call them ancestors.

These eyes are my grandfathers.
This tongue, a grandmother
I never knew.

Wildcat Strike

WV co. schools will not work . . . Barbour, Berkley, Boone,
Braxton, Brooke, Cabell . . . will not work. WV co. schools
will not work, today . . .

Teachers: Jennifer, Donna, Pam, Anne, Pat, Anita,
Tina, and Judith dress in red t-shirts silk-screened
outlining counties in the state, a slogan that reads:
#55 United.

. . . WV co. schools will not work . . . Calhoun, Clay,
Doddridge, Fayette, Gilmer, Grant, Greenbrier . . .
will not work. WV co. schools will not work, today . . .

Made with leftover teaching supplies, purchased
out-of-pocket, they hold signs that read:
I teach my students to stand up for themselves.
Here's my real-life example—#55 United, 55 Strong
without union leadership authorization,
support, or approval. *The power of the people*
is stronger than the people in power.

. . . WV co. schools will not work . . . Hampshire, Hancock,
Hardy, Harrison, Jackson, Jefferson, Kanawha . . .
will not work. WV co. schools will not work, today . . .

State Attorney General Morrisey warns a strike
of *any length*—10 minutes, two hours, five days—
on any ground—school, state capital, street corner—

is illegal. His office will support district attempts
to enforce state bans on public employee strikes.
Gov. Justice tells teachers, *get back to the classroom*
or else, via Twitter, but signs a bill granting a 2%
pay raise that won't cover inflation.

. . . WV co. schools will not work . . . Lewis, Lincoln, Logan,
Marion, Marshall, Mason, McDowell, Mercer . . .
will not work. WV co. schools will not work, today . . .

At protest sites, students and parents join them
with homemade glitter signs that shine despite
overcast, asking, *we support our teachers, why won't you?*

. . . WV co. schools will not work . . . Mineral, Mingo,
Monongalia, Monroe, Morgan, Nicholas, Ohio . . .
will not work. WV co. schools will not work, today . . .

Unsanctioned and unmovable for eight days,
chanting—*55 strong, 55 united.* Arizona, Oklahoma,
California watch a state with little left to lose
dig its heels in. This is a lesson in organizing.

. . . WV co. schools will not work . . . Pendleton,
Pleasants, Pocahontas, Preston, Putnam, Raleigh . . .
will not work. WV co. schools will not work, today . . .

Standing at the intersection in Flatwoods, a concerto
of car horns throws support. Cold, tired—uncertain
if they'll have jobs tomorrow—still, they smile sincerely.
Anne snaps a group selfie to post on Facebook,
caption that reads: *holding down the home fort.*

. . . WV co. schools will not work . . . Randolph,
Ritchie, Roane, Summers, Taylor, Tucker, Tyler . . .
will not work. WV co. schools will not work, today.

Imagining themselves in correctional orange, possibly
transferred to khaki—printed, processed, a guard
calling them forward for mandatory federal delousing:
Inmates Miller, Warner, Wilburn, Johnson, Facemire, Lambert,
White, Knight, and Boyce, please step forward respectively.
How does one prepare for dehumanization?—
They're not far from the prison.

. . . WV co. schools will not work . . . Upshur, Wayne,
Webster, Wetzel, Wirt, Wood, and Wyoming . . .
will not work. WV co. schools will not work, today.

Yore

No matter
where
you bury
the bones,
the dogs
will drag
them
home.

Grave of a Chinese Laundress

Nowhere near the monument of the famed senator,
Nor the white lotus fingers of the French wife of Diss Debar,

Beyond wiry, amber grasses, in the same turn
That holds the baby's grave,

Beside the crouched lamb with cloven-feet
Tucked under its breast,

Is a slanting stone tablet with Chinese writing,
Glyphs stacked and arranged

Like tracks of winter birds,
Few know what the words say, except . . .

Here the earth held me once,
Just as the new moon holds the old moon

In her arms. Ten thousand miles I traveled,
Leaving steep, green mountains,

Abandoned the black, roiling waters
Of my birth,

To sweat and stir over
A boiling cauldron of banker's clothes,

On lower Ann Street, in Parkersburg, West Virginia.
The iron dragon of a steam press hissed,

As my aunt and uncle argued, clucked like birds,
I hid between the stiff corpses of men's starched shirts.

I was a girl with whips of black braids and a face as gold
As a lampshade at twilight.

Among the morning mist we would rise,
Those of us with Manchu eyes,

Singing in Mandarin, the discordant cords
Of a child plucking a string.

The Americans live on houses with rooms
As high as mountain cliffs.

There I pass an old woman left on the porch
In a wicker wheelchair eating a Bartlett pear.

Little black boys in britches taunt me,
"Yella girl, yella girl, how come you always

Go to work in your pajamas?" I pick up a stick,
Chase them. The boys yell, *"Go home, yella girl,*

They say you stink like butter."
The next day I run away,

Escape to the river
Threaded with the shadows of drowned slaves.

At the riverbank I hook a carp, a writhing, muscular
Thing that struggles against me like a human heart.

That night I break into a fever.
Pearls of sweat beading my brow.

There is a pounding, pounding, pounding upstairs
Yet there is no upstairs and still it pounds.

A man in a boat woven from dark reeds
Rocks against my cot. He places his hand on my forehead

And smiles. His face is a yellow lantern.
Do I follow him? *Yes. You must.*

Together we shatter the darkness,
As I lift from my ribs like a snowy owl.

Where do I go? My relatives bury me hastily up the street
In a graveyard among people who never learn to pronounce my name.

Many years I floated over this stone tablet, fine as mist,
A president walked over me once. Like me, he died too soon.

Eventually my brother came to retrieve my bones.
They say I cannot rest until this is done.

By stealth of night, he opened the ground to take me
As a single sunflower glowered over the iron fence.

My brother carried my bones home in a metal suitcase,
Where I joined *Gan Bao's Sous hen ji* in stories of the immortals.

There are no Chinese now.
No Chinese to sing songs of Mandarin.

High are the voices of ghosts, tender
As paper flowers, strong enough to wake the dead.

The Nails of Spring

Time to break from the dark asylums of winter,
As the hag beats her stick to wake the ground.
Time to brace the stinging winds,
As the ewe drops her lamb in the field,
Placenta steaming like a bear's heart.
It is time to leave our mother,
As nails rain down to spark earth's soil,
Where log bodies stir into life.
Tonight the lamb will pull
The stars across the heavens.
Tomorrow spring will come
Like the green skin of my death.

The Little House Where They Brought Me Home

Today it looks bombed,
More like a drawer, really,
Exploding with old clothes.

The cheap, brown siding which spells
"Poor" in Appalachia is still here,
Glittering like dirty teeth.

The recently-stripped windows are eyes
Ripped from their sockets,
As if to say "Leave no witnesses."

And the pump, here is the pump
Where water spilled its cold
Diamonds over my hands.

The crows which flew overhead
Were the black clothes of a prowler
Who stole into the house and took
The bride's gold watch from a bureau

In a room where they slept.
Somewhere it is still ticking
With the cruel astonishment
Of her bitter heart.

Over there is where the sleepwalker
Slipped off her wedding band,

And tossed it behind the broom
In a pile of swept dirt.

In the next room is where
The groom lay unconscious, his naked
Forearm like a bandage over his eyes,
Leaving the mouth uncovered as if he is
Praying for the godless, cursing at the dead.

Here is where the boy sobbed in his bed
When the drunk wrecked the Christmas tree.
Here is where the baby lay in her crib, and thought hard,
As light shoved its way through the drab curtains.

In a short time, this house
Will be no more than a boxcar flying
Out of the hills of the imagination.

Today none can remember waking up in the place
And there is nothing left to fear.

Teacher Liz Demonstrates a Fiddling Technique As She Recalls the End of Fiddlin' Bill Hensley's Grey Eagle Reign in Asheville, Circa 1930

When the last note peaked like the shriek of a woman
        from Fiddlin' Bill Hensley's *Old Old Calico,*
    smoke curled
from that devil's black bow.

And when the crowd rose to greet him
        in thundering stomping and applause,

they all knew he'd won that ten dollar prize, for the twelfth (or
    twentieth) time.

But then the man to challenge Hensley took the stage
        (the river slowed and women, men, and children *pricked
    their ears—)*

Uncle Aldie Smathers took a nod and parted waters with his bow.

Thin and tall, his hair combed back severe,
he could have been a preacher, prim and stalwart,
pickaxe nose and matching temper—

He let go
    an easy laugh
had practiced on this tune a solemn year
    to gain the sway of courage required
to take Old Man Hensley with his own tune.

It took two minutes to unstitch some twenty years
of Fiddlin Bill's "Grey Eagle" reign—

as Aldie's fiddling rose from the smokey ridges
of the *Blue*
    and *Black*
        whose lowdown guts—
Lake Lure to be exact,
gave up 70 12-inch rainbows
        that same day,
and *Chimney Rock* whose gullies plunged,
    released the mottled corpse of Jeffery James
who'd hitched a rail car all the way
from Braselton

        as if this confluence of Buncombe County light
and sound could lift him to the glory of applause

—where the audience, perched for the end—held on.

Where Aldie stood to take his prize,

a crisp, ten-dollar bill to hold forever on
    the bridge
of Fiddlin' Bill's nose.

Leaving the Old House

1. The Trap

If it's empty, the dab of peanut butter
whiskered but ignored, it's postponement
I'll have to bear. Or worse,
she's there, broken
at her neck or back, depending on
her size, or if she was tentative
or starved beyond repair.
And what about her mate?
(I caught them in the middle
of their act last night.)
When I've reset the trap,
and placed it where I should have
from the first, (the kitchen drawer's
proximity as feckless as that pair)
I'll hear the snap and know
his end came fast. No panic
in his small but right-sized heart.

2. The Grave

I don't think love dies with the body
shot in the mouth and burned to ash and
buried in a pine box on the hill above *Helber's Church,*
George and Isabelle painted on the transom,
our children digging for crawdads in the culvert
on the day we put you underground, the grave
squared off, plotted out, reserved,

my cursive *J* entwined with your *D*
making its way among the wild pea vine.

3. The End

Beyond the bed stripped clean,
sheets pulled from corners,
pillows tossed like bombs to the floor,
out in the dark, through the glass
lies The Queen in her Chair,
the outline of a woman

black between her legs and arms and crown,
the only sound, a dryer tumbling,
a full heart, nothing like a constellation
where we keep our better selves
for wishing upon.

4. Leaving the Old House

It's not the mice, the girl
an easy catch, her eyes perpetual in
What? Or, the other one, her mate

inclined to take the meal and run,
the trap flipped empty,
his tiny rifle fire to show he'd won.

It's not dreams of other men
I'd never do in life. The distant squirrels
who chew the wires inside my sleepy head.

Not morning sun that has no way inside
but through the cracks in shutters drawn,
tree branches, holes of shadow on the wall.

It's not regret that someone tried,
what anchored us to discipline and dream.
It's that you chose against kissing
this place goodbye. It's that you stay.
It's that you never thought
I might want something else, some kind of peace.

The thing you did in spite of truth:
the left-hand faucet cold, the right-hand, warm,
backwards, fool.

Shame

I just don't see the shame in loving what you've got, say,
a small pond as opposed to an ocean,
not even half an acre,
because loving a small pond, by default, is like loving
the small town I come from. Isn't love a metaphor
for all the excuses I have ever made for staying
where I'm most alive,
even if that means I don't know much about functioning
out there in the real world
of ideas?

Yesterday
I talked with an old friend. She left teaching
to become a therapist. We sat in her car and she asked me,
are you talking to me as a friend or a therapist because I can't really be
    your therapist.
It felt like a trick question. Like all of these questions I ask myself.

Light on a small pond makes me think
I am the center of the universe
like I have all of the advantages of floating in space,
not tied to anything,
but the shore is right there. Cattails,
nests in cattails, water iris, yellow
yellow water iris, carp rising to the top,
visible as fear.

It is possible to drown in a teaspoon of water
or choke on my own spit

when I bite into a plum so juicy I'm not ready
for that explosion in my mouth.

Small ponds are like small children,
they accept things as they are. There's always room for improvement,
    sure,
but I don't always want to work on that.

Do you feel shame? My friend asked me.
Of course I do,
I said. But the light was ending
and I didn't want to have to drive home in the dark
by myself.

Killing Off Friends

When Granny Blanche and Miss Rosalee got together,
people from their hometown died
or were resurrected at the drop of a hat.
What happened to So-and-so?
Isn't she dead?
No she's not dead! She lives with her daughter in Detroit!

I sat there giggling quietly to myself.
Older women have always been my role models.
I do not fear aging.
My friends and I are now reaching that *certain* age.
I wonder how long before we start
Killing off our friends?

The City Park Bridge

For Peter Ellsworth Bennett, 1880-1960

How was it then, for a man orphaned in 1890,
His youth worked away on the canals,
Cast adrift again by the Great Flood of 1913?

How was it then, nearly starved to feed his family,
Saved by the trains, roaring down the old tow path?
Tracks needing labor, switches needing lanterns.

How was it, nearly trampled by the Great Depression,
Until 1935, when government hope and money,
Gave pomp and ceremony, music and dancing,
The best of the man's work, offered as his gift?

How was it as he watched the celebration?
He who had labored to cut the stone, chipped, toted, and hauled?
His own ropey muscles dredged down to watery bedrock,
To lift up the solid graceful arches for the city park bridge.

Discernable Proof

Our fire wouldn't catch, so you tried
carburetor cleaner, sprayed it in a straight
line at the smoldering kindling. Ignition.
Flames shot so high and I worried our
eyebrows would catch, my contacts would melt.
Our children ran around the fire like tiny wild men,
their voices rising to the treetops.
I asked if roasting marshmallows on a fire
started with carburetor cleaner was a good idea.
You replied that it was better than when I started
one with the Restoration Hardware catalog.
The cleaner burned away, you said. The poison
rose up and away, gone quickly into the canopy.
I looked for some discernible proof: glowing
leaves or falling fireflies. Nothing.

After dark, after I'd given the dog what he
needed to make it through the noise,
after we'd wiped and re-wiped charred, sticky
marshmallow remains from the children,
we walked across the road with glasses of
wine and folded camp chairs
to Mt. Zion Cemetery.
I was skeptical that we would be able to
see the fireworks from the town downriver.
I was sure that hills would
obscure our view. I was wrong.
Color burst into the sky,
the children ran figure eights around tombstones

and I remembered why (even though quiet and rolling
and lovely) I'd always avoided the place. Your chair,
placed near a small, mossy stone. A lamb
perched on its top.

The sky silent and dark again, the smoke
rolling into the valleys,
we walked back to break the silence
in our own yard.
We put the children to bed, sat
under Orion's belt, finishing the wine,
watching the embers of the carburetor fire
shimmer and pop, doing just fine on its own,
fueled by wood from the sugar maple
we reluctantly cut in the spring.
I tick these things off in my mind:
the maple, the river, the stones, the children.
The things in the way, the things we fix
or can't fix. The proof that isn't always there.
I write this to remember that
we keep the fire burning.

Barbara Costas-Biggs

Trillium as Accomplishment

with a line from Jane Kenyon

I didn't start out down the path looking
for them, but there they were:
three white petals cloaked

in the loveliest green, pollen dusting
the leaves, six stamens pointing right
up at me. It was an accident, this time

I had salvaged to take a walk.
I wish I could sketch this flower
with a pencil on thick, uneven artist paper.

I would bring it back
to show you that I have accomplished
something: a drawing on paper

seems like something more, seems
like enough and better.
I walk home, toppling the grasses in the field.

Bordertown (A Menagerie)

Farmers' kids go off to college.
                    Revving engines dualie trucks Save-A-Lot parking lot
                    Friday night lights.
Mom ushers in this thought *you need to sign up for the ACT.*
                              I reckon Mom'll be at work late again.
                              Cross over the county line and the

vultures pick at a doe's drying guts as a combine harvester's jagged
fangs lead the way takes up the whole road beside lurching off to
another field of corn turned pale and skeletal asking for reaping
brittle bones

                              it's all brittle bones

It's all bones but different bones cross county lines differing incomes
differing considerations on the subject of stepping in mud

    they want to keep their boots clean people from outside town their
        big farm houses like castles watching acres and acres no trouble
                              besides the occasional brave coyote

                        in gulleys deep in the holler no sight too far
                              your house that's it
                    around the bend up the road the neighbors

        In the hills a turkey loosens up its throat lets out a gobble

A mother's warning *I better not hear you're out with those Ketchum
boys again future felons if they aren't already you've got your own future
to consider when dealing with those rednecks.*

Bunch of fucking yuppies in town
trying to pass a clean lawn ordinance fuck you if you think my lawn
needsta look any way I don't want it

Take into consideration the fact that all these well-off people can
shoot all the bucks they want during gun season, but ain't a one of
them gonna butcher it themselves.
Only reason they've got to recognize us down in the sticks.
That's why I can charge so much.

Need at least a 25 to get into Ohio State according to my guidance
counselor.

Lessons from the Edge of Appalachia

Ten tiny four-year-old steps from my house, the land between two shotguns gets no direct light except at noon. I run my small fingers around the edges of fire bricks that define a shadow garden. Lifting them from the soft, moist dirt and grass, I find pill bugs, worms and dewdrops hiding. This becomes my secret hiding place, my refuge.

At six, school bus rides along winding roads with wildflowers hugging the edges take me past pasture land where my daddy and uncles herded dairy cows in their youth, out Route 141 beyond the edge of town to Edmondson's Farm. The day camp meeting house has a tree growing right up the middle; we laugh and pretend it's Jack's beanstalk.

The creek there is filled with minnows and crawdads. My grandfather gives lessons about birds, bees, seeds and the union of all Creation. He teaches me that everything we do creates ripples rolling out in concentric circles from the source affecting our unseen future; he introduces me to the Plant People who heal us.

At nine, I ponder The Hill. Before dynamite blew it apart to create a shortcut between Chicago and southern beaches, the sandstone bluff defined the northern edge of town, shifting from sort-of-a-city to the really rural county where children wait in tall wooden sheds for the bus that will carry them to school. I walk four so-called city blocks to mine.

At ten, I achieve the same rite of passage as my daddy did: I find a snake stick longer than I am tall, peel it, and carve in my initials.

One Saturday, after polishing my mother's house, I am dismissed to roam from Eighth Street to Tenth at the foot of The Hill. Climbing zigzag, the slope behind the armory and orphanage is relatively easy. I know the trail; I've gone up with others older than myself. This time I travel alone.

A brown penny sack holds a boiled egg and pbj sandwich for energy; the canvas-covered metal canteen slung across my chest is filled with icy water, enough to carry me up and back. In summer heat I enjoy the cold radiating on my hip and learn to swish the liquid against the edge of my throat, careful not to drink too much so I can remain decent in public. I do not perspire in the delicate daughter feminine; climbing strenuously, I sweat like a working man.

Up I go, over the tunnel on Route 93— an old Underground track and the way to Vesuvius Furnace that clad Old Ironsides in the Civil War, Pedro the home of musician Bobby Bare, and the runaway rendezvous called Blackfork. I climb all the way to the flat rock where an anonymous somebody has carved the initials JR.

Feeling satisfied and accomplished, I sit with feet dangling and gaze over my end of town, past the edges of the Ohio River into Kentucky. Watching barges ply the greasy ribbon of water, I enjoy my success and think about how far my people have come and contemplate how far I will go.

Filled with possibilities, I come down expertly dodging bushes, branches and briars. With home in sight, I drink until thirst is quenched. I hear my inner self tell me that I have passed the test. I have conquered The Hill all by myself.

I do not know then that I am one of the last to do so.

Erica Manto Paulson

Crossing the Edge in November

Driving across the big waters between Ohio and Kentucky,
a semi truck crammed full of young turkeys pulled in front of me—
a hundred or more beautiful birds stacked one on top of the other
in crates across the bed of the truck. You can imagine how ashamed

I felt, it being almost Thanksgiving, I knew where they were going
and I couldn't help but notice newly flecked, brown feathers
just starting to come in under the downy white covering their bodies;
the blue gobbler of the males was beginning to protrude along
their necks—they were just old enough to be afraid. At some point,

whether you try to avoid it or not, you will be on the edge
of young and afraid, and you will see the body you crammed yourself
    into
was the vehicle that carried you across the midlife line of the only
living you had ever known. It's time to break free now, leave that shell

on the banquet table the world will feast upon, you know their
    hunger.
Become the body of grace and of truth. Be kind to yourself, like
    earth and sky;
be like the river you had only ever crossed over, back and forth so
    many times,
until now when you are submerged in the place where the lines
between things are not so clear—in the thin places where there is no
    sign
that says "welcome, you are home" and "you are leaving, goodbye."

Mother's Day, 1984

Go get your Grandma, *Mom sd,*
Park in the alley. Go now.

Go to the back door.
Get in quick and get out.

What's goin on? *I sd,*
What's the rush?

She's had trouble, *she sd,*
That bastard Cash Powell.

He's gone out for more liquor,
so go now. Quick in, quick out.

I kept an eye out from the alley
to the back door. I tried the
locked door then knocked.

A .38 Colt revolver peeled back
the door curtain, Grandma's
spectacled right eye behind the sights.

Her left eye opened
when she recognized me.
The curtain fell back.

The safety chain rattled,
slide lock clicked free,
the deadbolt unlatched.

The brass knob turned,
door flung open and she
pulled me into the kitchen.

She glanced in the yard,
locked the deadbolt,
set down the gun.

What's goin' on, *I sd*,
What's he done now?

Nearly killed me again, *she sd*,
Shot at the back of my head

while I was fryin' bacon.
Look, *she sd*, over the stove.

One bullet hole was wide right.
She'd felt the other pass by.

He stopped shooting, *she sd*,
when bacon grease flew his way.

The Day Jerry Tolliver Killed My Saw

Siding the cabin, I shouted lengths
while Jerry made the cuts

Six boards to go,
something broke loose

inside the saw
as he finished a cut.

What the cowboy hell
was that? *I sd.*

It's your cheap-ass saw, *he sd.*
Somethin's rattlin' inside.

He tapped the trigger
to test it. I cringed.

Let me take it apart, *I sd.*
Maybe we can fix it.

No time, *he sd.* It's Date Night,
I gotta get back to the house.

It got worse with each cut.
After the third board

he tried to shake it out.
On the fourth, it caught fire

but Jerry forced it
through the end of the board.

I'm done, *he sd*. I'll come back
when you get better tools.

Felco #2

I hone the curved
cutting edge—
three passes of a
diamond whetstone,
squirt a drop of oil,
work the action
so the pruner springs
open, lock it closed,
push it inside the
worn leather holster.

These thirty years it's
made a million cuts—
daffodils, dogwood,
honeysuckle,
asparagus, apple,
peach, pot,
juniper,
Japanese maple,
bailing twine,
the tip of my thumb.

The red handles, a
match to my right palm,
put me in mind of the
Swiss gardener, sitting
alone at his bench,
forming the die and
casting the metal

to fit my hand
years before
I was born.

Saying It*

After Gwendolyn Brooks

Words form themselves like glass shards in my
mouth, no place to rest my tongue. It's best
to spit them out fast. Hold no fixed allegiances.
Some say the past lives on in us. Some are
wrong. A memory is not a hand cupped to
your sleeping breast. No flame against the
cold. So say it then. Dead.

*A "golden shovel" from a line from Gwendolyn Brooks

This Is Not a Drill

It's true I was mostly schooled between bomb threats;
no need to squeeze my big girl limbs beneath
my ink-scratched wooden desk, scaled
to a generation less fleshy than my own,
and everything bad that happened

happened somewhere else, behind curtains
of iron (which I confused with lungs
made of the same dull metal), to children
whose monthly allowance did not trust in God—
those heathen babies we lit candles for.

My cousin died playing in a cardboard box.
His neck snapped back and I never saw him again.
But even he was a country cousin
with gravel instead of a lawn.

And so I am trying now to squeeze myself
into the shoes of my poetry students, to walk
the crisscross mile of their hallways and stairwells,
wondering who's on the other side of the lockdown door.

One told me no way should they give teachers guns—
you can never tell who's going to snap. Another needed all
the fingers on her one hand to show the times she'd faced a gun
outside her house, the other hand for home.

They really ought to check my backpack, she told me.
I don't know why they think it won't be me.

Nothing Startling*

When it comes to the mining company and
it comes to the worker, production is all there
is. It's all there ever was.
How much dust I suck in? How long I'm going to live? Nothing.
Someone else is there to take my place. There's no startling
the rock dust from my lungs. No finding the heart in
the company. There's no cut long enough to reach the
seam. You want something to change, you might try to change the
    weather.

*A "golden shovel" from a line from Gwendolyn Brooks, using words from former miner
Harold Sturgill at the West Virginia Black Lung Association conference, June 2019

Goods Not for Sale

It is good to rise in the morning,
in the country, your neighbor's
stove smoke ghosting the shreds of dawn
that silver down through the trees. It is good
to have survived long enough
to know that pain may fade in time.
It is good to speak plainly, when life is
sweet water to drink.
It is good to have places like this
to remember when away: old barrels,
tractors rusted a velvet red
in fields of blooming ironweed,
the glimpse of an Amish girl, her dress like a hanky
waved in the wind, her face full of
honesty and light.
        It is good to wake at midnight
to the song of a mockingbird, or the *harr*
of an owl far over the hill. It is good
to know that thunderstorms can clean the soul.
It is good to have been given
years of homely music: the tinny gripe
of the pump, the snort and gurgle of the sink drain,
the *zee zee zee* pizzicati of katydids
in the cherry tree. It is good
not to owe anything for all of this:
enough to breathe, listen, be.
                And it is good
not to have lived too long in the country.
One grows old like the trees, and lightning

is waiting. Even the broom sedge, in winter,
cuts at the shins. Frost knocks on the doors
of the knees. The city offers gifts
of crowds and fervor and movement. Stillness can be
fearful. Even the traffic lights' come and go
is an invitation. Shop fronts shimmer and bloom,
day winks and goes on.
Even out on the sidewalk, though hustle
hawks its hurry every hour, though
all seems hapless Heraclitean change,
every pigeon now is every pigeon ever.

Men At Work

—old mill towns in Appalachia

In a clatter of collapsed beams,
bent steel, smashed masonry, gravity piling on,
cranes and derricks grub rubble with crab-clawed
buckets, plumbing the wreckage,
raising a deep blue diesel racket.
Smashed lockers, open hearths, chemical tanks,
blasted offices from which
sheaves of nulled contracts tumble and spill—
each crane's new hoisting leaks down-gyves
of falling debris. Smoke lurks. Dust billows.
Angle iron squalls and contorts. Hell
has come.
          But then, exactly at noon,
workers crawl out of their high machines
or rusting crow's nests of scrap
and ladder down to flat remains
to break out lunch buckets and thermoses.
Hardhats cast aside, they flip on their MAGA ballcaps.
After, they smoke leisurely in the wreckage,
as if disaster is a daily event, no more surprising
than a ringing phone, as if ruin is their native landscape,
mountains of junk and rubble,
valleys of veed girders and tangled wire,
landscapes of waste and loss,
forests of burned metal through which small streams of coolant
and steaming seepage from custodians' closets

and wrecked break-room vending machines
trickle steadily downward,
fishless, toxic, all the wrong colors
for sky, or water, or blood.

Ohio River Benedictions

after Pauletta Hansel's "A Blessing for the Feast of All Poets"

For the flight of the
    Great Blue Heron,
and after, its stilty
    watchfulness ashore,
        grazie.

For the trill of spring
    peepers on early March air,
    merci.

For the dried mudslick gilding
    the old lock guidewall,
    danke.

For uncanny words
    with which to
sing the names
    of clams and mussels: Catspaw,
Three Ridge,
    Ohio Pigtoe, Monkeyface,
Purple Wartyback,
    muchas gracias.

For the simple letters
    that make such words,
for *s* and *g* and *b*,
    for *t* and *c* and *e*:
Praise. Thanks. Glory.

OUTDOOR AND ENVIRONMENTAL WRITING

Northern Appalachia is home. The people and the communities of this region are connected in many ways through our shared struggles, frustrations, fears, triumphs, and hopes. We are connected through those who walked these mountains before we were born: our ancestors. We are even connected through our diversity, as counterintuitive as that may seem. Perhaps the strongest connection we share with each other as northern Appalachians, however, is with the land on which we dwell. The lush greenery that stretches from the fields to the mountains instantly evokes a sense of serenity, a sense of place, and a sense of home. The vibrant colors on the leaves in autumn and the blankets of snow painting our landscape white during the winter months are all comforting and familiar to us. There are times of extreme weather, of course, but it is always tempered in time. This, another lesson from our region, has taught us patience and perseverance.

The land has shaped us. All one needs to do to feel the influence of the environment of northern Appalachia is to step outside. Take a walk into the foothills. Travel the dirt roads. Find a long-forgotten trail. It is here that we can find our roots—our home. It is here that we are most connected to what it is to be northern Appalachia.

The culmination of this inaugural issue of the Northern Appalachia Review has woven a tapestry of our region, and the outdoor pieces serve a beautiful and important purpose. It is fitting that they are placed at the end of the journal, as Ben Moyer's complete piece *Fraxinus Lost* and the following excerpts bring us home, back to the land. Within these words, seeds have been planted. By reminding us of our connection to the region, the following authors have watered these seeds, which will certainly grow, blossom, and multiply in forthcoming editions of this journal.

In his essay, *Peace at Snyder Point*, Richard P. Hanlon Jr. skillfully articulates the sense of community that he observes while venturing outdoors in northern Pennsylvania. His thoughts explore this gift that Appalachia has shared with him and he ponders how these feelings and revelations can be extrapolated onto other areas of life. In the following excerpts, the author takes us on a journey and gives us a glimpse into the sense of awe and wonder that is stirred within him while he traverses the wilds of northern Pennsylvania.

One of life's greatest treasures for me is the sense of community that I feel in wild spaces. A saunter through field and forest, along the canyon rim or up a rugged mountain trail makes me feel like the wealthiest person in the world. There are moments when I'm convinced that this is true; when the busyness of life gives way to the tranquility, power, and joy of wild spaces; when, immersed in the full beauty of wild spaces, all sense of self is lost and paradoxically I find out more about who I truly am in those special moments.

. . . I ascend through hardwood forest and then higher on, into the land of dwarf juniper where exposed sandstone cliffs reveal the contours of ancient riverbanks. I take a short rest on the sandstone cliffs above Little Fourmile Run where golden beams illuminate vibrant moss and polypody fern on rocky cleft while Pine Creek flows on into eternity far below.

. . . I'm drawn into the most incredible sense of community. What great joy it is when the song of the winter wren bursts forth from these wooded ravines! It seems that one has staked his claim on the ravine just beneath Snyder Point, its voice amplified by the contours of these rock walls! I have to pause for a moment upon hearing the winter wren's song. There's something that feels extra special about the song of this little wild neighbor. To me the song of the winter wren is like the Angelus bell of the forest. In the 11th Century the Angelus bell was rung to mark special times of prayer in villages and monasteries. All of the people would stop what they were doing and stand in a moment of reverence or silent prayer while the bell was being rung. . . . The song of the winter wren is . . . my call to be present, to rest in the presence of God in community with my wild neighbors, and to welcome the gift that God has for me in this moment. It's no wonder that Jesus preached about love, forgiveness, and peace on mountains and along lakeshores. How could I possibly maintain a grudge in such a sanctuary as this? How could I possibly nurture hate in such a place? The flow of grace is especially profound here, inviting a renewed sense of spiritual awakening time and again.

. . . Near the end of every retreat into wild spaces, I always reflect on this gift. Here in the Pine Creek Gorge I feel as Muir did in his beloved Sierras, having developed a oneness with this wild space. I've come to know this lush canyon community and its many diverse inhabitants as neighbors. Henceforth, my wellbeing is dependent upon the wellbeing of this special place. It is a space of refuge for my soul and of connection with my wild neighbors who call it home.

Zack Buck's essay, *Thoughts from Deer Camp*, gives us a different sense of community—one that is shared amongst hunters in northern Appalachia. He explores the memories that are created amongst men while spending hours in the solitude of the outdoors. The following excerpts showcase how comradery is built, and with that, why nostalgia inevitably follows. The author reminds us of the community that our picturesque region of Appalachia has afforded us throughout the generations.

The deer camps are strange things. Amalgams of buildings and people. Musty smelling cabins that spend most of the year as the homes of field mice and chipmunks, but spark to life when rifle season comes about. Window sashes are thrown open, and hot, crackling fires are started in iron stoves to drive out the damp air. . . .

The deer camp was old even when the men were young. They stay up late telling stories and trying to recapture "the good old days." . . . The men needed less sleep and could eat more bacon and eggs than they can now. The crick ran deeper, and there weren't so many people on the mountain. You could see more stars in the good old days. The "buck pole" was always full . . . the hunters seem to remember they all stayed longer and had fewer worries waiting back home.

They spent more time laughing, lying, and playing cards, with the cigars and pipes putting off blue tendrils of smoke that gathered into thick clouds on the low ceiling. The spirits they drank warmed the bones better, with less side effects, back in the good old days. The men used to come in from the hunt with excuses why a shot was missed and had their shirt tail cut off in penance. Now, it seems most of the excuses are why no shot was taken: "let that one grow another year." It used to be that any antlered deer was considered a trophy. The noble defeat of a worthy quarry on his own terrain. Stainless guns with no soul now stand in the place once filled with walnut stocked rifles, gleaming with oil, silver showing through the bluing from being carried in buckskin gloved hands. Things were better when the laurels were shorter, and before the apple tree fell.

It seems the mugs of coffee tasted better before they dug the new well, and that a thermos of soup stayed hotter in the good old days. The bones creaked less, and the rifle sights were clearer. After all their years have been spent yearning for the earlier times when everything was black and white, save the grey winter skies, they think maybe they remember times that never were. The deer camp is a feeling, as much as a place. A feeling the men miss even as they sit inside the cabin's walls.

—Heather Moser, Editor, Book Reviews, Interviews, and Literature of the Outdoors and Environment

Fraxinus Lost

By Ben Moyer

A reluctant dawn seeps above Laurel Ridge's stark silhouette. I'm in my chair beside the window and before the woodstove, where my coffee cup squats on the warming rack before accepting its bitter, enlivening brew. Yellow light beams through the stove's glass doors, burnishing every surface it strikes.

I'm glad for the heat and aroused by the light, but without the contentment I've long taken from burning wood in my home. This heat and light carry out of my stove the taint of loss. They are the heat and light of ash wood, and I may be among the last firewood burners on these ridges to bask in its bright combustion.

Yet, I accept this fire's tempered pleasure and burn all the ash I can; might as well. From what I see, and by the official word of the forestry bureau, every sizable ash across these slopes is dead, and though their wood has many qualities, durability after death is not among them. Even standing dead in the woods, as millions now do, ash succumbs fast to weather and rot. Either I burn this unwelcome glut now, or see it decay into duff.

Ash's die-off happened so fast, across such an expanse, that it's unsettling. If you know our woods here, if you're attuned to their slow successional change and take reassurance in some degree of permanence there, it's terrifying. But to say that ash died off is not correct. Ash was done in by the emerald ash borer, a metallic-green beetle you'd be excused to mistake for a streamlined, space-suited grasshopper.

The emerald ash borer is a well-named but clandestine killer. The shiny-green beetles are harmless to an ash tree for the month or so, centered on May, they exist as adults, except that females lay eggs in bark cracks and fissures. The translucent, grub-like larvae that hatch from those eggs, then burrow inward, are what wring life from an ash tree. They mine under the bark through the tender sapwood, boring serpentine tunnels that entomologists call galleries. If the invasion of larvae is dense enough, as it has been inside ash trees across the Ohio Valley hill country and the Alleghenies' western slope, the galleries intersect and overlap around the tree's circumference, looking like ancient runes, strangling the tree.

No emerald ash borer ever chewed through an ash trunk here before about 2005. *Agrilus planipennis* is native to China, whose northeastern forests are elegantly like our Appalachian woodlands, with analogous plants and insects that fit niches, fulfill roles, we'd recognize from our own sylvan experience. The difference is that China's several ash species evolved in the ash borer's presence, devising biochemical defenses, enlisting allies, to blunt and balance its crafty attack. As a sudden alien in North America, the borer faces no enemies here, so our ashes stand open to onslaught.

The borer spends more than 300 days out of sight, under the bark, in a furtive strategy that helped it get here, hitch-hiking inside the grain of ash-wood crates or palettes shipped in with imported, must-have, merchandise—wide-screen TVs, perhaps. The first one identified in North America was caught among ash trees in a park in Canton, Michigan, near Lake Erie's western tip, in 2002. From there, the invasion exploded southward and east, engulfing urban groves along the Great Lakes, leapfrogging through Ohio Valley woodlots, and ascending the Alleghenies. Except for the epicenter in southern Michigan, no region became more saturated with emerald ash borers than our North-Appalachian uplands.

Depending on how finely you divide the taxonomy, either five or six ash species grow here, all of which belong to the genus Fraxinus—white, green, blue, black, red, and pumpkin ash. Red ash and green ash are genetic variants, sometimes considered the same species. Except for blue ash, which, like Asian ashes, manufactures tannin in its leaves so is less palatable to leaf-nibbling, egg-laying adults, all our ashes face the same internally girdled fate.

Green and white are our dominant ashes. They can be difficult to tell apart, but each has its favored conditions. Our western Allegheny foothills were "made for" green ash (*Fraxinus pennsylvanica*). Fast-growing, it likes sun and rich but well-drained soil, and thrives, too, along the sinuous corridors of sluggish streams. Consider those habitat likes, then recall the most significant land-use change across hill-country Ohio, western Pennsylvania, and panhandle West Virginia since the mid-20th century—abandonment of farmland. Green ash has flourished here in the wake of old crop fields and pasture, surging up idled valleys and spreading over neglected hills.

White ash (*Fraxinus americana*) is a tree of upland forest, standing there with oaks and maples, and gains prominence over green ash as Allegheny ridges steepen to the east. The blue ash (*Fraxinus quadrangulata*) can be found in those high woods too but is less common than white. Our other "minor" ashes claim limited niches in wetlands, on river islands, or floodplains. Given ash's prevalence here, wherever an adult emerald ash borer winged south from Michigan, it could land on an Appalachian ash tree.

I remember the first time I learned about the borer. It must have been around 2006 or '07. I'd seen—couldn't miss—a purple kite-like contraption, just bigger than my RFD mailbox, hanging in a tree in Ohiopyle State Park. I puzzled over the thing, then forgot it, but soon saw others, which prompted inquiry. These, I learned, were "prism traps" (the traps are triangular when viewed from either end), placed by the U. S. Dept. of Agriculture and the state Bureau of Forestry to monitor the emerald ash borer's initial advance into western Pennsylvania. Borers are drawn to purple color, and a pheromone lure inside the trap attracts adults to a sticky surface where they're caught and marooned. The purple snares were reassuring. "Well, at least we're on top of this early," I remember thinking. But no one, not even forest pest professionals, could envision the quiet ferocity of this assault. Within three years of those traps' hanging to detect pioneers, ash trees around here declined, then died. Entomologists acknowledge now that, because the borer larvae live beneath the bark for 11 months, grubs might have been mining through ash sapwood before the traps made their first capture.

Ash in mind and hand

Helplessness attends any attempt to describe a living ash tree's appearance—in the way that you can't summon up a friend's face after she has died. Peterson's Field Guide to Trees and Shrubs says ashes are tall trees of symmetrical form, with an oval crown and trunk that sub-divides low, a truth that can still be seen among the standing casualties. But look quick, as the decaying branches are falling away fast. Just give thought to where you stop to rest in the woods on windy days.

A sure way to know an ash is to examine its juxtaposition of parts. All components of an ash tree are arranged as opposites. Twigs erupt opposite one another from larger branches, and the compound leaves likewise oppose their neighbor across the stem. All ashes have compound leaves, and even the leaflets are opposite their counterpart along the leaf's petiole. Ashes are our only tree whose leaves are both opposite and compound, so the dual verification is foolproof. Look close at a dead ash, stark and bare. This theme of opposites is easy to trace throughout its form.

Ash foliage, if I recall, had a lacy look in summer, owing to its compound leaves. There is still time to learn to know the bark, though it, like the branches, is shedding away from the standing boles. On trees old enough to develop their signature pattern, the bark looks like parallel rows of steel chain running up the trunk. The links in the chains are ridges enclosing diamond-shaped basins. Examine the bark now and you'll notice it's peppered with holes shaped like a "D," about the diameter of a pencil eraser. The Ds mark places where an adult beetle emerged from its larval gallery under the bark.

I see now that, before the borer, I never noticed how much ash was in the woods, how common it had been in its vigor. I'd walked among ash all my life, sat at their bases watching for deer, placed a hand upon them in passing, without apprehending their spread. It's impossible now to overlook them. They stand out as pallid cadavers, peppered over with woodpecker pits, their bark sloughing off in 6-foot slabs, piling into spongey pyramids at the base. Somehow, I had tended to think of ash as a mid-size tree, rarely rivaling the big oaks or beeches. But now that they're gone, and that search-image of pallor and rot is ingrained in my brain, I stumble upon lifeless giants I'd failed to wonder at in their prime. What had preoccupied me so when I passed near this massive tree in the past? Is my mind capable of accommodating only the search for morels, or a deer's flicked ear, in a moment outdoors? Certainty that I would have admired these tall ashes had I known their end was near affords scant solace. So, I content myself with the warmth and light from their disassembly in my stove. I've made a ritual of it, a private homage.

When I awake and rekindle my fire, I feed the stove with ash splits only. I arrange the splits over the night's surviving coals, open the vent all the way, then sip coffee and study the burn unsullied by the flames of other fuel.

At my first sips, the coals dim as the added wood absorbs their heat, cooling the stove's interior. But before I'm halfway through the cup the ash-stack brightens at its base. Before I pour my second, flames are licking the undersides of lower splits. The ascending blaze kindles a slab, claims a foothold, then hops up to the next undersurface, as if climbing a staircase from beneath.

Flames rising out of ash wood are yellow, clear, and steady. They never sputter and they throw no sparks. My stove ticks and groans from its expanding parts but the wood burns quiet, as if it were a fuel for stoves first and, secondarily the once-living tissue of a tree. As the splits torch, their flames burn uniformly across their lengths, with no flares like those that burst from black cherry. Those cherry flares erupt from pockets of resin trapped among the fibers. Ash's combustible molecules must be evenly spread along its grain without clumps or pockets, yielding this stable burn. Propane gas would behave this way, I imagine, if compressed into a bar I could carry and stack.

This steady burn may be linked in some molecular way to ash's quick surrender to the stroke of my maul. When I drive it down into a broad round of ash, the head burrows in with a satisfying cleave. Even if the round is too big to split in one blow, a straight rift shoots down the outside and I'm encouraged. I know one more stroke will do it. I set myself, lift, drive, then torque my wrists on impact. The round vaults apart into two equal halves, with none of the tearing and shred characteristic of oak. Suddenly exposed, the new surface is the color of bread scarcely toasted.

Like all seasoned wood, ash has its own fragrance, strongest in the moment you rend it apart. Ash's scent is simple and clean. "Salt" comes to mind, but I'm not sure that's right, and the sense of salt is fleeting. If I press my nostrils to the new surface, I can prolong the aroma but not for long. It's pleasing but elusive, like stepping into a fresh-painted room you've returned to admire, before your nose grows accustomed.

Ash wood is light for its volume, and straight of grain, both traits long noted. "Fraxinus," the generic name for all ashes, translates in Latin as "spear" or "javelin," and the common name has roots in the old English "aesc," which meant "spear" or "lance." Light but strong, ash wood must have been prized as shafts for weapons that, for better or worse, shaped western civilization. I'll likely never wield an ash-shafted spear, but I can apprehend the qualities that lent this wood to that purpose. When I get my ash splits down to kindling size, I can grip the maul's handle close to the head and part the wood into springy strips with a flick of my wrist. The kindling leaps apart with pent-up strength that once begged some soldierly use.

Splitting ash into kindling reveals another of this wood's qualities, less martial but equally prized. As my maul drives downward, a clear tone rings out from the parting bonds, oddly entertaining to hear. Sometimes, I give in to impulse and experiment with this tone, splitting pieces of varying sizes, and wielding the maul at different rates to play a crude tune at my splitting stump, noting the pitch ascend as the strips grow smaller. I'm no musician, but when I learned that ash wood is prized for making electric-guitar bodies, because of the way it enhances sound, I felt affirmed in this whimsy. If you attended a baseball game in the time before the borer, you've heard this signature ring from ash too. That gratifying "crack of the bat" pealed out of the spring of ash wood, long preferred for bats because its light weight allowed a batter's swing to achieve its highest velocity in the split-second his mind perceived the flight of the ball. Since the ash borer's march across mid-America, most bats are made from maple, hard wood but it lacks ash's resilience. If you watch a game today, you'll notice how often maple bats explode in batters' hands.

After ash

A notable truth about life in modern America is that there is no general acknowledgement of indigenous ecological loss. Righteous angst simmers for rainforest and polar bears, but there is little heed to our own native fabric's unraveling. State highway departments sometimes fell dead ashes along roadsides, so a crashing ash doesn't impede the traffic, leaving the wood to lie in the ditch. That's about it. You could saw the trunks into manageable pieces to pick up and use (I do) if you dared risk stopping along the shoulder, offending the careening cars even by slowing down to exit the stream.

There is, however, an unconscious mourning, apparent in every recent autumn. Weather forecasters, chambers of commerce, and tourism bureaus now annually note the "muted" fall foliage that disappoints visitors. Dry weather, wet weather, and late frost have all rationalized the deficient autumnal tint. But no voice ever proposes that the rapid disappearance of ash accounts for the drabness. Ash was dazzling in fall, wasn't it? Does memory serve me when I recall it as buttery-yellow, sometimes tinged around the edges with gauzy orange? Didn't it jump out to the eye, especially on overcast days? We may not have noted such radiance when it erupted before us every autumn, but we are aware of its absence, even if we cannot give a name to where it went.

Other repercussions go beyond the aesthetic. Landslides are part of this region's clay-soil geology and steep terrain. But these events are lately more frequent, complicating life around Pittsburgh's hilly perimeter. The television news reliably reports on these slides, noting frequent rains and saturated clay, both true enough. Video-feeds show the viscous mud, blocked highways, and teetering homes poised on the edge of suburban abyss. But never noted are jumbled piles of dead logs visible in many shots—ash logs to my eye—whose roots once knitted that hillside together, and whose death surrendered the slope to gravity.

When today's children grow up, without having known of ash trees, there will be an absence in their lives they have no way to sense. This strikes me as profound impoverishment, greater, perhaps, than the vanishing of ash itself. I and all those my age have lived in just that kind of vacuum left behind by American chestnut. Except for the stories and lore of "old-timers," I never knew this dominant climax tree of the Alleghenies, and I can't help but wonder what that void has meant in my life. But at least I knew that chestnut once lorded over these woods. Will children growing up today, in the wake of ash, even know such a lovely, useful tree once grew here in abundance? I can ask this question about children and ash because I did know ash in my time. I knew it direct and personal. I knew it connected to other things.

Ash in vivo

Sharp ridges wander across Greene County, Pennsylvania, embracing deep hollows in their weave, not unlike the chain-pattern of ash bark. Across many autumns, I would pick my way along the western slope of one such ridge, listening for the thrash of wild turkeys scratching in fallen leaves. A scatter of white ash grew among oaks and hickories across that slope. I knew where each one stood, and I eased through the woods from one to the next, knowing I'd likely find a flock beneath one ash or another.

Hunting this way is sublime pleasure. You are always moving, but slow enough to savor the fall woods' winey aroma, to feel on your fingertips the fine cellulose dust you can rub from the leaves' leathery gloss. By habit, I walk quiet in the woods, a challenge in dry leaves. As if by some grace, though, sounds of careful steps don't concern wild turkeys, especially if your gait is erratic, without the cadence of human ambulation. When scratching for a prized forage like ash seeds, turkeys make such a din themselves that an adroit hunter can approach a flock within shotgun-reach. When I'd done so, I liked to watch the birds awhile through the screening brush. I craved contact with their native, rural "rightness" in that place. Those birds belonged on that ridge, under the ashes. My deepest reward for hunting them well was the sense that I belonged there too.

After I'd watched the flock scratch and feed, I'd burst through the brush and run toward them at the best speed I could muster over rough ground, yelling, shooing, maybe firing off a shot in the air. The panicked turkeys sprinted and flushed in all directions, unleashing a riot of alarm "putts," to the tattoo of their stiff wings battering branches. As the birds escaped, a lingering shower of twigs and tendrils rained from the trees to affirm the chaos that had just happened, and I'd suck the chilled air for breath.

Such a disruption may seem odd, but scattering the flock is a traditional Appalachian way to hunt wild turkeys in the fall. In the days before game laws, when mountain people hunted out of need, a skilled and patient hunter could kill most of a scattered flock in a long afternoon. While the woods settled, I'd wait a quiet quarter-hour then stroke the wood-peg "striker" across the slate face of my call to fake a hen's assembly yelp. Social creatures, turkeys are desperate to regroup after such a fright, and if my calls rang true, unseen birds would yelp and "kee-kee" back from all directions. Soon, some would appear out at the limits of vision, dark and cautious, craning their necks, anxious to reassemble. And if I held motionless, they'd filter back onto the same scratched-up ground where I'd flushed them. Finally, I'd pick out one nice bird and end my hunt. So inclined, you could stay there for hours, calling more lonely birds back to the gun.

When I cleaned my prize for a feast, I'd open its crop, the pre-digestive pouch in the upper chest, to confirm what the birds had been eating. Each time I'd killed my turkey under an ash tree on that ridge, I could pull out a baseball-size wad of single-winged ash seeds, looking like the blades of canoe paddles,—"samaras" in botanical terms—the bird had scratched for and swallowed.

Ashes were reliable seed-producers, which is why I could find a turkey flock on that ridge every fall. But in recent autumns, unless it's a good acorn year and the birds are scratching beneath oaks, the ridge is silent, with no thrash in the leaves up ahead, no scratched-up duff beneath the remains of skeleton ashes, and a diminished lure to be there.

Innocence, boon, and hope

It may be no consolation that the rapid extermination of ash here is a case of ecological "what goes around comes around." The borer could never have spawned such hordes without a ubiquitous host, and ash could never have achieved the prominence it did across this region without radical alteration of the landscape by humans, long before the borer hit. Ash's wholesale crash was set in motion two centuries earlier when settlers cleared the Ohio Country of its diverse forest cloak for farmland, laying the groundwork for widespread dominance by pioneer species like green ash when that same land was later abandoned. Once the invader benefitted from its welcoming jump-start in green ash, its fortified billions found and infested the other ash species.

Still, it is important to dispel any sense that the emerald ash borer "destroyed" North America's ash tree resource, even any hint of that sense this writing may have conveyed. The ash borer did nothing apart from what it evolved to do, which is to feed from an ash tree's inner membranes, and to reproduce itself. Our ash catastrophe was a matter of context, in which the borer obeyed its internal mandate suddenly free of all balancing checks on its abundance, in an altered place where its host had done much the same thing, dominating idled farmland at the expense of a more varied forest less vulnerable to borers, because it could. Unless we accept the borer's innocence in our loss, we remain ill-equipped to intercept other catastrophic invasions.

All living things exploit opportunity, which is why, in nature, a collapse can elicit a consequent boon. When I was a boy, following my father, uncles and their bird dogs across the boulder-strewn slopes above the Youghiogheny River to hunt ruffed grouse, which were abundant then, we sometimes were treated to the sight of an even more striking big bird, its wings flashing black and white in undulating flight among big trees. More often, we'd only hear its clamoring "Yuk, Yuk, Yuk" call from some unseen haunt. But rarely, this bird would alight on a trunk within sight, bigger than a crow, and I'd admire its rakish red crest, watch it hammering at the wood at a pace mechanistically rapid, not possible from a flesh-and-blood creature. My elders called it the "Indian hen," which seemed fitting at the time. Later, when I found that bird described in some periodical, likely Pennsylvania Game News, I learned it was the pileated woodpecker.

For years after those encounters, I read that the pileated woodpecker was in steep decline and feared its "laugh" would be resigned to my outdoor past. Ornithologists pronounced the pileated "old-growth obligate," that it needed old timber to survive, especially the dead, cavity-riddled trees always present in mature forest. Wood-dwelling insects thrive in such systems, which woodpeckers excavate and devour. But, experts predicted, there was not enough old timber to sustain the big woodpecker, and the bird would vanish from American woods within a human generation.

Yet, if you go into any tract of woods in our region today, even wood-lots that checker farm regions, you are likely to see pileated woodpeckers prospecting on the boles of dead ash. Their numbers grew and their range ballooned over the past decade, in response to the numberless ash borer larvae they plucked from tunnels with a few raps at the decaying wood. In what's left of the ash woods you can hear their drumming from all directions, and the ground is littered with punky chips they've carved out with their beaks, leaving rectangular excavations along the trunks. Cavity nesters, pileated woodpeckers find perfect nest sites in those same pocked trees.

Even with their populations spiking, woodpeckers can't eat enough of the larvae to make a difference for ash, and the woodpecker irruption is likely temporary, a wave of birds following a wave of abundant forage.

I like to think about that image of a living wave, because within it glimmers a hint of hope for ash. Even if baseless, hope, in our time, is an alluring refuge for those attuned to the natural world.

No apparent pattern explains where this occurs, but at "random" places in or near dead ash woods, you will, even today, come upon vibrant stands of ash seedlings, high as your knees and dense as weeds. Sometimes these clumps crowd beneath the gray remains of their parents. In other places, no adult ashes are present, indicating that the massed deposit of wind-borne samaras blew in on the same gust together, and found suitable footing. Born of the last fruiting by lingering ashes, these natal clusters stand lanky as ginseng stalks, too gaunt to attract a female borer intent on egg-laying, and with too little girth to harbor larvae. They are hard to spot in winter, but in summer the pale-green compound leaves betray them, beckoning you to check closer for their opposite orientation of leaf and twig, which proves them to be what you hoped. Once your eye learns to spot these seed-beds, you'll notice others, and your dream that ash trees may yet be part of our place here will soar.

A tempting prospect leaps to mind when you encounter such a trove. Maybe the ash borer will over-achieve here, eat itself out of existence. Maybe, with all the ash trees big enough for a borer to bore killed by mastication, it will die out for lack of hosts and be gone. Then, these persevering seedlings could grow unmolested, mature, and loose their own seed to the wind.

That may be a naïve vision, rooted less in rationality than in yearning. I have read no ecologists' judgements on this possibility, and when I encounter some informed treatise so directed, I may likely avoid its conclusions. I'd rather be able to hold onto hope.

BOOK REVIEW

Reviews not only serve the purpose of raising awareness of various literary works, but they also give insight into an author's personality and writing style. Reviews are as invaluable for the reader as they are for the authors who are being discussed. It is for this reason that we wanted to incorporate this genre in the journal.

In our inaugural issue, we are fortunate enough to include a review of Nancy McKinley's *St. Christopher on Pluto*, which takes place within northern Appalachia. Our reviewer, Sara Pisak, is a northern Appalachian herself and therefore is able to give us a unique perspective on McKinley's work. The primary goal of the Northern Appalachia Review is to highlight stories of and authors from the region. Sara Pisak fulfills this goal with the following review as we get a glimpse of how McKinley represents this area, the culture, and its people in her book, along with hints of the entertaining and relatable themes present within its pages.

—Heather Moser, Editor, Book Reviews, Interviews, and
   Literature of the Outdoors and Environment

St. Christopher on Pluto is *Thelma and Louise* with a surprising third wheel: a small Saint Christopher statue affixed to the dashboard of "Big Blue," a Buick Regal left to MK by her grandmother. Through fifteen interconnected stories, Saint Christopher guides MK (Mary Katherine—but don't you dare call her by her formal name) and her elementary school friend, the ever-outspoken Colleen, as the women reconnect years later, working at the destined-for-bankruptcy Keystone Mall in their small, northeastern Pennsylvania town.

From MK's dash, Saint Christopher sees all: from Colleen ditching her broken-down car and reporting it stolen, to MK and Colleen helping divert a protest outside a soldier's funeral. As the friends drive, a full portrait of their lives, personalities, and reverence for their town begins to emerge. McKinley's writing shines when she highlights the protagonists' personalities and has their juxtapositions swerve and curve around each other (like the backroads "Big Blue" navigates) but never collide.

MK is reserved and sarcastic; Colleen is outgoing. A self-described "Celtic Warrior," she is constantly volunteering MK for adventures and sometimes fraud. Together they must find the strength and faith to push forward as their lives seems to stall, as Big Blue sometimes does.

Being stalled is a matter of perception, and, as MK says, "So much depends on the frame of perception." Unlike Thelma and Louise, MK and Colleen never leave their hometown and the surrounding areas. Their identities and friendships are interwoven with their relationship to their hometown. Small hometowns, like those in northeastern Pennsylvania, present a duality based on perception. Someone might see lack of economic growth, people either fleeing or getting left behind, and a failure to branch out. Others, like MK and Colleen, see long-standing traditions, work ethic, and a familiarity to create their own opportunities.

Never pigeonholing her characters or their homes into hollow stereotypes, McKinley highlights the hope, comfort, and creativity these individuals and their hometowns exude as they are touched by AIDS, war, aging, sexism, race, religion, family dynamics, immigration, and poverty. *St. Christopher on Pluto* stresses that tending to hometown roots is not stalling or idling; it is cultivating a system that, like roots, we might not see or understand how far-reaching they are. MK says it best: "The more I thought about leaving here, the more I realized I didn't want to go. I've got roots here."

McKinley's use of individual yet interconnected characters to slowly reveal hometown appreciation makes the reader profoundly care not only for the characters, but also for a town which others might have deserted. As St. Christopher watches from Big Blue's dash, he teaches: the places we stay in, the places we return to, and the places where we put down roots are more meaningful than all the destinations we simply escape to or visit. MK and Colleen don't need to drive across the country and into the Grand Canyon to realize that it is rich personalities, like theirs, that make these places rev with life.

—Sara Pisak

EDITORIAL STAFF BIOS

Fiction Reader: Hannah Allman Kennedy

Hannah Allman Kennedy grew up among the oil ghost towns of Venango County, PA. She earned her BA in writing from Geneva College, and is an MFA in Creative Writing Candidate at Carlow University in Pittsburgh, where she teaches writing and has completed residencies in Pittsburgh and at Trinity College in Dublin, Ireland. Hannah has worked as a freelance writer and editor for the past five years. She lives in Pittsburgh with her husband, Alex.

Fiction Reader; Social Media Manager: Samantha Backstrom

Samantha Backstrom is a Pittsburgh native who has a BA in English from Clarion University of Pennsylvania and an MA in English Literature from John Carroll University, where she has published poetry in the John Carroll Review. She returned to Pittsburgh to take a position as an adjunct English and Study Skills Instructor for the Gussin Spiritan Division at Duquesne University. Samantha also serves as an adjunct English Instructor at Carlow University. She is currently working on her MFA in Creative Writing at Carlow University, with a concentration in Fiction.

Assistant Poetry Editor: Kathleen S. Burgess

Kathleen S. Burgess is senior editor, *Pudding Magazine: The Journal of Applied Poetry*, and served the Ohio Poetry Association as vice-president. She juried for and tours with Women of Appalachia Women Speak, critiques with Poetry Salon Columbus (co-chair), Bistro Poets, and the Southern Ohio Writers Collaborative. Her poems and interviews appear in *North American Review, Sou'wester, Main Street Rag, The Examined Life, HeartWood, r.kv.r.y.* Burgess won a Sheila-Na-Gig 2018 poetry prize and other national and state prizes, and she has four Pushcart Prize nominations and two Best of the Net nominations. Her poetry collections include *Shaping What Was Left* and *Reeds and Rushes—Pitch, Buzz, and Hum*—editor (both Pudding House); *Gardening with Wallace Stevens* (Locofo Chaps); *What Burdens Do Those Trains Bear Away* (Bottom Dog Press); and *The Wonder Cupboard* (NightBallet Press). The retired public school music teacher and her husband Jack Burgess live in Chillicothe, Ohio, amid Hopewell earthworks in the Appalachian foothills. Visit www.kathleensburgess.com.

Nonfiction Editor; Poetry Reader: Carrie Hohmann Campbell

While Carrie Hohmann Campbell has an MFA from New York University, she never strayed too far from the hills along the Allegheny River. She teaches composition and creative writing at Edinboro University of Pennsylvania and has published two chapbooks. Her work has appeared in *Salt Hill, Sixth Finch,* and *Forklift Ohio*, among others.

Fiction Editor: Damian Dressick

Damian Dressick is the author of the story collection *Fables of the Deconstruction*, forthcoming (CLASH Books) and the coal country novel *40 Patchtown* (Bottom Dog Press 2020). His fiction and essays, many of which deal with the lives of working people in northern Appalachia, have appeared in more than fifty literary journals and anthologies, including, most recently, *W.W. Norton's New Micro, Post Road, New Orleans Review, Cutbank, Hippocamps,* and *HeartWood Literary Journal.* A Blue Mountain Residency Fellow, he holds an MFA from the University of Pittsburgh and a PhD in Creative Writing from the Center for Writers at the University of Southern Mississippi. Damian currently teaches at Clarion University, and lives in western Pennsylvania. Damian has been described by Frederick Barthelme as "an artist to be reckoned with." He has also been described by his eight-year old daughter as "a writer with extremely poor penmanship." He can be found online at www.damiandressick.com.

Poetry Editor; Submissions Manager; Production Consultant: William Scott Hanna

A life-long resident of the Upper Ohio Valley, William Scott Hanna is an Associate Professor of English at West Liberty University in West Virginia where he teaches creative writing and American and Appalachian Literature. Having generational family roots in Northern Appalachia from Pennsylvania to Ohio to West Virginia, the region, its culture, and its literature have become primary interests in his scholarship and his creative work. After finishing his PhD in American Literature with a dissertation that focused on the contemporary American poetics of place, he began to focus more seriously on his creative writing. Over the past few years, he has published poetry and creative nonfiction in a number of print and online journals, including *Pine Mountain Sand and Gravel, HeartWood Literary Magazine, Fourth and Sycamore, Cleaver Magazine, Belt Magazine, and Still: The Journal*. He lives with his wife, son, and daughter one block from the banks of the Ohio in Wheeling, WV.

Editor, Book Reviews, Interviews, and Literature of the Outdoors and Environment; Nonfiction Reader: Heather Moser

Heather Moser is an adjunct professor in Classics at Kent State University where she received her MA in Latin Literature. Her areas of study include moral panics, particularly related to the Bacchic cult during the Roman Republic and the European Witch Craze of the 14th-17th centuries, the fluctuation of Julius Caesar's memory throughout history, the preservation and transmission of Appalachian folklore, and lore related to and evolving from cursed objects. She has published several short stories and poems and served as guest editor for the *Crossroads* issue of the online speculative poetry journal *Eye to the Telescope*. She has authored chapters in interdisciplinary academic books such as *Private and Public Voices* and *Evil Women*. Diving into her northern Appalachian roots and folklore of the area, Heather has served as a guest author and narrator for the *Thirteen Past Midnight* podcast. An ongoing contributor to the Weird Writer blog for *Into the Fray Radio* podcast as well as *The Caravan,*

Library of Lore, her work covers folkloric elements from different time periods and cultures. Heather is also a researcher for the film production company *Small Town Monsters*, assisting with films such as *The Mothman Legacy* and *The Mark of the Bell Witch*.

Founding Editor and Editor-in-Chief: PJ Piccirillo

PJ Piccirillo's fiction and articles have appeared in magazines, newspapers, syndicates, and journals. He has twice won the Appalachian Writers Association Award for Short Fiction. His acclaimed novel *The Indigo Scarf* (Sunbury Press/Brown Posey) won Brown Posey Press's 2019 SUNY Award. *Heartwood* was published by Middleton Books. An artist-in-residence for the PA Council on the arts, PJ has worked with thousands of students in many genres of composition, and he has partnered with visual and film artists in cross-discipline projects, including a televised documentary. He has long advocated for the under-recognized literature of northern Appalachia, dating to his stint as a commonwealth speaker for the Pennsylvania Humanities Council when he traveled the state presenting *Missing Pages: the Neglected Literature of the Alleghenies*, which made a case for a canon of northern Appalachia authors. Surly about the lack of a support network for writers of the region, PJ founded the Writers Conference of Northern Appalachia. An instructor of English and Humanities at Butler County Community College, he holds an MFA in creative writing from the University of Southern Maine and a BA in English from Saint Francis University. PJ is a third-generation volunteer firefighter, an EMT, and a professional firefighter for NASCAR. He otherwise can be found with his wife and three sons pursuing all things outdoors on the creek-fissured plateau of his native northcentral Pennsylvania.

Fiction Reader: Virginia Rafferty

Virginia Rafferty is a bestselling author of historical fiction focusing on immigration from Eastern Europe in the nineteenth and twentieth centuries. Informed by genealogy research, family traditions, and a trip to Slovakia and Hungary, she has written two novels, *Family Secrets...Hidden in the Shadows of Time* (2015), followed by *The Road to Lattimer* (Sunbury Press, 2019). Virginia is a retired middle school science teacher with an M. Ed. from Antioch New England Graduate School in Keene, New Hampshire. She is a member of the South Carolina Writers Association, Aiken Writers' Bloc, and volunteers at the McGrath Computer Learning Center.

Fiction Reader: Nicole Ravas

Nicole Ravas has a BA in English from Marymount University and an MA in Interdisciplinary Education from Santa Clara University. Originally from the Washington, D.C. area, she lives in Pittsburgh with her husband, her son, and their two dogs. She is an executive assistant and adjunct instructor at Carlow University, where she is pursuing an MFA in Creative Writing with a fiction concentration. Prior to working at Carlow, she was a K-12 English teacher for 13 years. In her free time, she is a freelance editor.

Fiction Reader; Web and Marketing Consultant: Dan Reidmiller

Dan Reidmiller is a writer based in Pittsburgh, Pa. He graduated from Chatham University's MFA CW, Fiction, program with a concentration in Pedagogy, and works full-time as a Content Writer/Strategist.

Fiction Reader; Administrative Coordinator; Production Coordinator: Debra Reynolds

Debra Reynolds is a writer, blogger, dreamer and voracious reader who has always lived in the wilds of northern Pennsylvania. A self-professed Grammar-Nazi, she can be found on Facebook at *The Promiscuous Reader*. She has had articles, short fiction and one poem published locally and online. In addition, she spends time advocating for disability rights with emphasis on autism, epilepsy, and elder care. She often writes on the difficulties particular to rural areas, especially health care access and services. Other interests and writing topics include travel, gaming, handicrafts, and the unique and beautiful character of the region she calls home.

Poetry Reader: Matthew Vargo

Matthew Vargo lives and writes in Pittsburgh, PA. He is pursuing a creative writing MFA at Chatham University and has publications in the National Gay & Lesbian Review as well as two Write Volumes Anthologies, *Shades of Horror* and *Shades of Transformation*.

Nonfiction Reader: Cheryl Werber

Cheryl Werber works in the human services field as an executive administrative assistant and among other things is a freelance writer. She earned her bachelor's at the University of Pittsburgh and her masters at Carlow University. She wrote for *U.S. News & World Report, CDA News*, and *Parachute*, MapQuest's blog. Cheryl writes creative non-fiction and fiction, is a workshop facilitator for Girls Write in Pittsburgh and is the Board Secretary for the ToonSeum, a museum that champions comics as a force for social good through education while cultivating more inclusive audiences.

Copy Editor: Rita Wilson

Rita Wilson is an English and creative writing teacher, a writer, and an artist. She has won several awards for her artwork, and her art and writing have been published in *Rune* and *Riverspeak Literary Magazines*, wolfmatters.org, and *Voices in the Attic*. Rita earned her MFA in Creative Non-Fiction from Carlow University in 2015 and subsequently published her first book, *Greek Lessons: A Cultural Odyssey*, which also includes photos of several of her paintings. A recent retiree from public education, Wilson has taught adjunct at the University of Pittsburgh and has given writing workshops in both creative writing and professional writing. She spends her time painting, writing, traveling, and playing and coaching tennis. Wilson resides in the suburbs of Pittsburgh with her husband, son, dog, and cat.

Brook/Macmillan in 2017 and named an Amazon Book of the Month. His poetry collection, *Believe What You Can*, was published by WVU Press and won the Weatherford Award from the Appalachian Studies Association and was also named Appalachian Book of the Year by the Mountain Heritage Literary Festival in Tennessee. His poems have been anthologized by Kent State University, the University of Iowa, University of Georgia, and University of Arizona. He is the seventh poet laureate of WV and was recently named co-winner of the 2019 Allen Ginsberg Poetry Award.

Gerry LaFemina's latest books are the poetry collection *The Story of Ash* (Anhinga, 2018) and a new chapbook, *Points South* (Hysterical Books, 2019). A new volume of prose poems, *Baby Steps for Doomsday Prepping* (Madville, 2020), is forthcoming. His previous books include a novel, a collection of short stories, and numerous award-winning collections of poetry, including *The Parakeets of Brooklyn*, *Notes for the Novice Ventriloquist* (prose poems), *Vanishing Horizon*, and *Little Heretic*. His essays on poets and prosody, *Palpable Magic*, came out on Stephen F. Austin University Press and his textbook, *Composing Poetry: A Guide to Writing Poems* and *Thinking Lyrically* was released by Kendall Hunt. He has also written a novel (*Clamor*), a collection of short stories, and numerous pieces of creative nonfiction. Among his awards and honors is a Pushcart Prize, A Michigan Council for the Arts and Cultural Affairs Fellowship, and an Irving Gilmore Foundation grant. A noted literary arts activist who has served on the Board of Directors of the AWP and edited numerous literary journals and anthologies, LaFemina is the former director of the Center for Literary Arts at Frostburg State University where he is a Professor of English, serves as a Poetry Mentor in the MFA Program at Carlow University, and is a current Fulbright Specialist in Writing, Literature, and American Culture.

Nancy McKinley is an award-winning author of fiction and nonfiction. She earned her Ph.D. from Binghamton University, receiving the John Gardner Newhouse Award; MA from Colorado State University; and

BA from College of the Holy Cross, where she was one of the first females at the previously male school. A founding faculty member for the low-residency Wilkes University Maslow Family Graduate Program in Creative Writing, she teaches fiction and nonfiction and supervises the writer-as-teacher internships. Her novel-in-stories, *St. Christopher on Pluto* (West Virginia University Press, 2020) is set in the northern brow of Appalachia.

Nearly fifty of **David Poyer's** novels and works of creative nonfiction are in print with major publishers. He has also published oral history, travel, and biographical nonfiction, and has collaborated on memoirs. Poyer has been translated into Japanese, Dutch, Italian, Hungarian, and Serbo-Croatian, and rights have been sold for films. Writers he has mentored have been taken on by major literary agencies, published by major houses, appeared on New York Times Top Ten bestseller lists, won the International Latino Book award and other prizes, and become college teachers. His latest is *Overthrow*, published by St. Martin's/Macmillan in December 2019. He teaches at Wilkes University.

CONTRIBUTOR BIOS

Latif Askia Ba

Latif Askia Ba lives in Brooklyn, NY but studied at Edinboro University, majoring in Computer Science with a minor in Mathematics and Creative Writing. It wasn't until he went away to school that he discovered a passion for literature and language. His first chapbook, *Wet Monasteries*, was published by the Erie-based magazine Alien Buddha Press.

Joseph Bathanti

Joseph Bathanti, son of a union steelworker and union seamstress, respectively, grew up in Pittsburgh. He is the former Poet Laureate of North Carolina (2012-14) and recipient of the 2016 North Carolina Award in Literature. He is the author of ten books of poetry, four books of fiction, and two books of nonfiction. Bathanti is McFarlane Family Distinguished Professor of Interdisciplinary Education & Writer-in-Residence of Appalachian State University's Watauga Residential College in Boone, NC.

Roy Bentley

Roy Bentley, a finalist for the Miller Williams prize for *Walking with Eve in the Loved City*, is the author of eight books, including, most recently, *American Loneliness* from Lost Horse Press, who is bringing out a new & selected in 2021. He has published poetry in *Crazyhorse, december, The Southern Review, New Letters, Shenandoah, Blackbird, Prairie Schooner,* and *Rattle* among others.

Robert Beveridge

Robert Beveridge (he/him) makes noise (xterminal.bandcamp.com) and writes poetry in Akron, OH. Recent/upcoming appearances in *Red Coyote Review, Deep South Magazine,* and *Aromatica Poetica*, among others.

Daniela Buccilli

Daniela Buccilli's chapbook is *What it Takes to Carry* (Main Street Rag). Her poems can be found in *Pennsylvania English*, *Coal River Review*, *Paterson Literary Review*, *Cimarron Review*, and *Italian Americana*. She holds degrees in teaching and writing from Penn State, University of Pittsburgh, and Carlow University. She has edited the anthology *Show Us Your Papers* and teaches high school.

Zack Buck

Zack Buck is a lifelong resident of the Canyon Region of Pennsylvania. He was raised as a woodsman and hunter, spending as many as two-hundred nights a year under the stars before settling down with his wife Tracy and starting a family. He now spends his days as a custom rifle builder and raising his children to be as wild as he was.

Omope Carter Daboiku

Omope Carter Daboiku grew up in the southern Ohio river town of Ironton. Her writing focuses on the intersectionality of place, identity and belonging, and the experience of growing up a "mixed-race, colored child" on the Appalachian landscape. After 30 years in Cincinnati, she now resides in Dayton, where she enjoys five rivers but has found no hills worth climbing.

Jodie Childers

Jodie Childers received an MFA from Brooklyn College, and has published prose, poetry, non-fiction, and photography in literary journals such as *The Portland Review*, *Enizagam*, and *Poetry East*. Most recently, she published "Appalachian Apophenia" in the collection *Appalachian Reckoning: A Region Responds to* Hillbilly Elegy, as well as academic articles about American cultural history, folk and punk music, literature, and self-taught art. She received the Himan Brown Award, the Dorothy Sargent Rosenberg Award and was awarded 2nd place in the Ledge fiction contest. She is completing a feature length documentary film on Pete Seeger's environmental legacy.

Greg Clary

Greg Clary is Professor Emeritus of Rehab and Human Services at Clarion University, Clarion PA. His poems have appeared in *The Rye Whiskey Review*, *The Watershed Journal*, *Trailer Park Quarterly*, and *North/South Appalachia: Poetry and Art, Vol 1*. His photographs have been published in *The Sun Magazine*, *Looking at Appalachia*, *Tiny Seed Journal*, *The Watershed Journal*, *Hole in the Head Review*, *Dark Horse*, *Trailer Park Quarterly*, and *North/South Appalachia*. His book, *Piercing the Veil: Appalachian Visions*, with Byron Hoot, was published in 2020. He was born and raised in Turkey Creek, West Virginia, and now resides in northwestern Pennsylvania.

Barbara Costas-Biggs

Barbara Costas-Biggs lives in Appalachian Southern Ohio and works as an academic librarian. Her work has appeared recently or is forthcoming in *Glass*, *8 Poems*, *Riggwelter*, *Ghost City Press*, *Literary Mama*, and others. She has an MLIS from Kent State University and an MFA from Queens University of Charlotte.

Tom Donlon

Tom Donlon lives with his wife and children in Shenandoah Junction, WV. He earned an MFA in Creative Writing from the American University in Washington, D.C., before moving to West Virginia in 1986. He was awarded a chapbook, *Peregrine*, in November 2016 from a book contest sponsored by the Franciscan University in Steubenville, OH. Poems have appeared in many journals, newspapers, and anthologies. Recognition has included Pushcart Prize nominations and a fellowship from the WV Commission on the Arts.

C.Dubielak

C. Dubielak has lived and worked in Appalachian Ohio since 1983 as a writer and visual artist. Her work has appeared in the *Mid-American Review*, *Plainsong*, *Riverwind*, *Jitney*, and *Pikeville Review*, among others. She makes her home in a former Catholic church in southern Perry County, Ohio.

Donna Dzurilla

Donna Dzurilla is a graduate assistant in Carlow University's Creative Writing MFA program and specializes in fiction. Her novel-in-progress follows the lives of a family during and after the decline of the steel industry in Pittsburgh. Donna's work has appeared in *The Penny*, several of the *Voices from the Attic* anthologies, and the *Pittsburgh Post-Gazette*.

Matthew Ferrence

Matthew Ferrence is the author of *Appalachia North: a memoir*, recognized in 2019 as Book of the Year by the Northern Appalachian Writers Conference, and *All-American Redneck*. His essays and short fiction have appeared widely in North American literary journals, including *The Fiddlehead, Gettysburg Review, Colorado Review*, and *Best American Travel Writing*. He lives at the confluence of the Rust Belt and Appalachia, where he teaches creative writing at Allegheny College.

Christina Fisanick

Christina Fisanick, Ph.D. is an associate professor of English at California University of Pennsylvania, where she regularly teaches expository writing, creative nonfiction, and digital storytelling. Her work has been published in a variety of magazines and journals, and she regularly contributes to *Weelunk, InWheeling*, and the *Wheeling Intelligencer*. In addition, Fisanick has written and published 35 books, including her most recent memoir, *The Optimist Food Addict* (MSI 2016). She lives in Wheeling, West Virginia.

Mike Franchioni

Mike Franchioni lives just outside Pittsburgh, PA, doing much of his poetry reading and writing on the daily bus commute downtown, the scenes and characters he encounters often informing and inspiring his writing. He is active with the Allegheny Valley Poets, and participates in readings around the city.

Jane Ann Fuller

Jane Ann Fuller's poetry appears in *Aethlon, Atticus Review, B O D Y, Fifth Wednesday, Grist, jmww, Pikeville Review, Rise Up Review, Shenandoah* (James Boatwright III Prize), *Still: The Journal* (forthcoming in June), *Sugar House Review, The American Journal of Poetry, Waccamaw*, in the anthologies *Women of Appalachia Project* and *All We Know of Pleasure*, and elsewhere. She co-authored *Revenants: A Story of Many Lives* with a grant from the Ohio Arts Council.

Michael Garrigan

Michael Garrigan writes and teaches along the banks of the Susquehanna River in Pennsylvania. He loves exploring the river's many tributaries with a fly rod and hiking the riverlands, and strongly believes that every watershed should have a Poet Laureate. You can find more of his writing at www.mgarrigan.com.

J.r. Gill

J.r. Gill is a poet and essayist based out of Columbus, Ohio. He was born and raised in Greenfield, Ohio, along the invisible line that separates the Midwest from Appalachia. His upbringing instilled a deep love for the rolling hills of southern Ohio. He is a student of Dr. Hunter S. Thompson.

Scott Goebel

Scott Goebel is a poet, teacher, editor and Swarper. He edited Jim Webb's *Get In, Jesus* (Wind 2013) and co-edited Joe Barrett's *Blue Planet Memoirs* (Dos Madres 2017). He lives above a bar near the Ohio River and docks at mile 466.

Lilace Mellin Guignard

Lilace Mellin Guignard raises kids in Tioga County, PA where she teaches creative writing, outdoor recreation leadership, and women's studies at Mansfield University. She is the author of *When Everything Beyond the Walls is Wild: Being a Woman Outdoors in America* (Texas A&M University Press 2019), and her poetry has appeared in *Poetry* magazine. Her website is www.tentofonesown.com

Kari Gunter-Seymour

Kari Gunter-Seymour's second collection, *A Place So Deep Inside America It Can't Be Seen,* is forthcoming from Sheila-Na-Gig Editions April 2020. Her poems can be found in many fine publications and on her website: www.kariguntermourpoet.com. She is the founder and executive director of the "Women of Appalachia Project™" www.womenofappalachia.com and Immediate Past Poet Laureate for Athens, Ohio.

Richard Hague

Richard Hague was born, grew up, and worked in Steubenville, Ohio. He is author or editor of 20 collections of prose and poetry, a recipient of The Weatherford Award in poetry, four Ohio Arts Council Individual Artist Fellowships in two genres, and a scholarship to Bread Loaf. He continues as Artist-in-residence at Thomas More University in northern Kentucky.

Richard P. Hanlon Jr.

Richard P. Hanlon Jr. is an ordained elder in the United Methodist Church. Rich received his Master's Degree from Pittsburgh Theological Seminary and his Environmental Studies Degree from Penn State Altoona. He considers himself a lifelong student of Jesus and of wild spaces. Rich manages his blog, www.BestLife.Community, and leads wildlife tours in the wild spaces near his current appointment.

Pauletta Hansel

Pauletta Hansel is author of seven poetry collections, including *Coal Town Photograph* and *Palindrome*, winner of the 2017 Weatherford Award. Her writing has been featured in journals including *Rattle*, *Appalachian Heritage* and *Still: The Journal*, and on *The Writer's Almanac*, *American Life in Poetry*, *Poetry Daily* and *Verse Daily*. Cincinnati's first

Poet Laureate, Pauletta is artist in residence at Thomas More University, in her home state of Kentucky, and is managing editor of *Pine Mountain Sand & Gravel,*. More about her writing, writing workshops and retreats can be found at https://paulettahansel.wordpress.com/.

Kathryn Holt

Kathryn Holt is an illustrator from Wheeling, West Virginia. She holds a Bachelor of Fine Arts in Illustration with a minor in printmaking from Edinboro University of Pennsylvania. Kathryn works in a variety of artistic mediums, including pen and ink, scratchboard and collage. Combining various found objects, artistic mediums and illustrations, her collages focus on capturing the nostalgia of childhood memories.

Alison Condie Jaenicke

Alison Condie Jaenicke teaches writing and serves as Assistant Director of Creative Writing at Penn State University. Her work has appeared in such journals as *Hippocampus; Superstition Review; Gargoyle; Storyscape; Brain, Child;* and *Literary Mama*. Her essay "I Slept Well If You Slept Well," published in *Isthmus*, was recognized as Notable in *The Best American Essays 2016*. Find her online: https://alisoncjaenicke.weebly.com/

Mark Sebastian Jordan

Mark Sebastian Jordan is a refugee of the corporate world, which he left in 2005 to concentrate on writing. He has written plays, humor, history, poetry, and music criticism, and has received an excellence award from the Ohio Arts Council. He lives in the Appalachian foothills of Holmes County, Ohio.

Stephanie Kendrick

Stephanie Kendrick is an Appalachian woman from Southeast Ohio. She is a village council-woman, case manager, and Brazilian Jiu Jitsu blue belt, as well as a mother, wife and daughter. She has had the honor of being published alongside other Appalachian authors in *Women Speak: Women of Appalachia Project's Anthologies 4 & 5, Sheila-Na-Gig, Ghost*

City Review, Not Far From Me: Stories of Opioids and Ohio, and *Essentially Athens.*

Kip Knott

Kip Knott's poetry has recently appeared in *The American Journal of Poetry, Barrow Street, The Ekphrastic Review,* and *Virginia Quarterly Review.* His most recent book of poetry, *Tragedy, Ecstasy, Doom, and so on,* is forthcoming from Kelsay Books. Currently, he is a teacher and an art dealer living in Delaware, Ohio. More of his work can be accessed at www.kipknott.com.

Cathy Lentes

Cathy Cultice Lentes is the author of a poetry chapbook, *Getting the Mail* (Finishing Line Press, 2016), and she holds an MFA in Writing from the Solstice Program of Pine Manor College near Boston. Her work has appeared recently in *Essentially Athens: A Celebration of Spoken Word and Fine Art,* and *Feminine Rising: Voices of Power and Invisibility.* www.cathyculticelentes.com.

Margo Orlando Littell

Margo Orlando Littell is the author of the novels *The Distance from Four Points* and *Each Vagabond by Name,* which won the University of New Orleans Publishing Lab Prize and an IPPY Awards Gold Medal for Mid-Atlantic Fiction and was named one of fifteen great Appalachian novels by *Bustle.* That story was based on actual events that occurred when traveling thieves appeared in the area in the early 2000s. Margo received an MFA from Columbia, and her work has been nominated for a Pushcart Prize. Originally from Connellsville, Pennsylvania, she now lives in New Jersey with her family.

Michael Lockett

Michael Lockett is an MFA Candidate at Carlow University. He is a former Peace Corps Volunteer who served in Mauritania, West Africa and works as a mental health professional in Pittsburgh. Michael's childhood in northern Appalachia resulted in distinguishable details that appear in his characters' traits and settings. He resides with his partner, three cats and two birds in the Northside. This is his first published story.

Barb McCollough

Barb McCullough has split her time between teaching and writing in WV and OH. While a WV educator, Barb worked as a WV Humanities Scholar and as an OSU Asian Studies Fellow. Barb collaborated with Marietta College as editor, grants writer, and readings coordinator. During 2018–2020, Barb traveled and read with Women of Appalachia Speaks collective.

Abby Minor

Abby Minor lives in the ridges and valleys of central Pennsylvania, occupied Lenape land, where she works on poems, essays, quilts, and projects for reproductive justice. The granddaughter of Appalachian tinkerers and Yiddish-speaking New Yorkers, she is Bitch Media's 2018 Writing Fellow in Sexual Politics and the author of the chapbooks *Real Words for Inside* (Gap Riot Press) and *Plant Light, Dress Light* (dancing girl press).

Ben Moyer

Ben Moyer's writing on nature, outdoors and conservation appears in numerous regional and national publications. His work has won Excellence in Craft awards from the Outdoor Writers Association of America and the Pennsylvania Outdoor Writers Association. Moyer strives to convey the value of personal connection to place, in his case Northern Appalachia, while interpreting scientific concepts and the region's natural history.

Erica Manto Paulson

Erica Manto Paulson is a poet whose work has most recently appeared on Dayton NPR, and in the upcoming *Dayton Anthology* by Belt Publishing. A lifelong Ohioan, Erica finds inspiration for her poetry in the fertile fields of her home state, drawing on a deep connection to the surrounding world and the "holy-ordinary" of everyday living. Erica is also a doula, teacher, birth activist, audacious optimist, viola player, and a hopeless dreamer. She resides in Centerville, Ohio with her husband and their large blended family of seven children.

Sara Pisak

As a reviewer, Sara has a first place award from the Society of Professional Journalism and is employed at Glass Poetry. While earning her MFA in nonfiction, Sara has published reviews in *Five: 2: One Magazine*, *Mookychick*, and *Yes Poetry*. When not writing, Sara can be found spending time with her family and friends. You can follow her writing adventures on Twitter @SaraPisak10.

David Prather

David B. Prather is the author of *We Were Birds* from Main Street Rag Publishing. He studied creative writing at Warren Wilson College. And his work has appeared in several journals, including *Prairie Schooner, Colorado Review, Seneca Review, Poet Lore, The American Poetry Review, Sheila-Na-Gig, Grey Sparrow Journal,* and others. He resides in Parkersburg, WV.

Vicki Pritchard

The author Vicki Pritchard is a Registered Nurse, still working part-time at the age of 75 years. She is a member of the Southern Ohio Readers and Writers Collaborative and has participated in readings and events throughout the southern Ohio area.

Bonnie Proudfoot

Bonnie Proudfoot resides in Athens, Ohio. Her fiction and poetry have appeared in the *Gettysburg Review, Kestrel, Quarter After Eight*, and other journals. Her short story "Old Spirits" won first prize in the 2020 *Sand Hills Literary Magazine* competition, and her novel, *Goshen Road*, was published in January of 2020 by Swallow Press.

Rachel Roupp

Rachel Roupp is a poet from Pennsylvania. Her work has appeared in *Crab Fat Magazine, Persephone's Daughters, Honey & Lime, Rust + Moth, Rag Queen Periodical,* and *Chantwood Magazine.* She is a graduate of Mansfield University and the recipient of the 2019 Sand Hills Prize in Poetry. She just wants Dolly Parton to be proud of her.

Barbara Sabol

Barbara Sabol's second book, *Imagine a Town,* was awarded the 2019 Sheila-Na-Gig Editions poetry manuscript prize. She is the author of *Solitary Spin* and two chapbooks. Her poetry has appeared widely in journals and anthologies. Awards include an Individual Excellence Award from the Ohio Arts Council. Barbara contributes book reviews to the *Poetry Matters* blog. She lives in Akron, OH.

Karen Scott

Karen Scott, poet and substitute teacher in Columbus, Ohio, is a member of Ohio Poetry Association and Salon Columbus poetry workshop. Her work has been published in two volumes of the Women of Appalachia Project anthology *Women Speak*; three issues of the OPA anthology Common *Threads*; and *Delirious: A Poetic Celebration of Prince.*

Susan Sheppard

Susan Sheppard is a nataive Appalachian with deep roots in West Virginia. She was the winner of a West Virginia Department of Culture & History's poetry fellowship early in her career. She was the first runner-up in the *Poets & Writers* Maureen Egen Writers' Exchange for 2019 and has recently been traveling as a part of the "Women of Appalachia Spoken Word Series." Her poetry has appeared in many literary journals, including *Nimrod, River Styx,* and *Ohio Review..* Among her poetry honors are the Edgar Allan Poe Memorial Poetry Prize in 2005, the Sri Chinmoy Award for Spiritual Poetry, the In Pittsburgh Prize, and the Yaddo Award.

Smagacz, Geoffrey

Wiseblood Books published a short collection of Geoffrey Smagacz's fiction, *A Waste of Shame and Other Sad Tales of the Appalachian Foothills* in 2013. The book won the 2014 Independent Publisher gold medal for Mid-Atlantic Best Regional Fiction. Geoffrey's poetry has also been published in *Dappled Things, 14x14, Mountain Mist (Appalachian Authors Guild Anthology)* and *The Society of Classical Poets.*

Elizabeth Solsburg

Elizabeth is a native of Scranton, Pennsylvania and is a graduate of the University of Michigan and Loyola University, New Orleans. Her poetry has appeared in *Next Line Please, Prompts for Poets and Writers*, David Lehman and Angela Ball, eds.; *The Avalon Literary Review; The Huron River Review; The Bear River Review; American Scholar Magazine*; and *Rat's Ass Review,* among others.

Judith Sornberger

Judith Sornberger's poetry books are *Practicing the World* (CavanKerry), *I Call to You from Time* (Wipf & Stock), and *Open Heart* (Calyx Books). She's also the author of five chapbooks and a prose memoir *The Accidental Pilgrim: Finding God and His Mother in Tuscany* (Shanti Arts Press). She lives on the side of a mountain outside Wellsboro, PA, among bobcats, bears, and deer.

Andi Stout

Andi Stout is an Appalachian writer from West Virginia. She is the author of Pushcart-nominated *Tiny Horses Don't Get A Choice.* Andi's poems have appeared in *Connotation Press: An Online Artifact, The Longleaf Pine, Junoesq,* and *Still: The Journal.* She earned her MFA at WVU in Morgantown, WV. Andi is an Assistant Teaching Professor in English at Penn State.

Jacob Strautmann

Jacob Strautmann's debut book of poems *The Land of the Dead Is Open for Business* is available from Four Way Books. Awarded a 2018 Massachusetts Poetry Fellowship by the Massachusetts Cultural Council, Jacob Strautmann's poems have appeared in *Agni Magazine, Forklift, Ohio, Salamander Magazine, The Boston Globe, The Appalachian Journal, Southern Humanities Review, Appalachian Heritage,* and *Quiddity.* www.jacobstrautmann.com

David Swerdlow

A finalist in the 2019 National Poetry Series competition, David Swerdlow has published two books of poetry with WordTech Editions: *Bodies on Earth* (2010) and *Small Holes in the Universe* (2003). His poetry has appeared or is forthcoming in *The American Poetry Review, Poetry, The Iowa Review* and elsewhere. He teaches literature and creative writing at Westminster College in New Wilmington, Pennsylvania.

Patricia Thrushart

Patricia Thrushart lives in the Wilds of Pennsylvania. She has published two books and her work has appeared in *The Watershed Journal, North/South Appalachia, Tiny Seed, The Avocet, Still Point Arts Quarterly, The Pittsburgh Post-Gazette, Feminine Collective, Curating Alexandria, High Shelf Press* and *PENNESSENCE.* In 2019, she won the NFSPS Diamond T contest. Find her at www.patriciathrushart.com.

Bernadette Ulsamer

Bernadette Ulsamer earned an MFA from Carlow University where she is a member of The Madwomen in the Attic. She is the author of the chapbook, *Trestling,* published by Flutter Press. Her poetry has appeared in *Pittsburgh City Paper, The Main Street Rag, Cossack Literary Journal, Roar Magazine, The Broken Plate, Meat For Tea: The Valley Review,* and has been anthologized in *Voices from the Attic,* and *Along These Rivers.*

Antonio Vallone

Antonio Vallone is associate professor of English at Penn State DuBois, poetry editor of *Pennsylvania English,* founder of MAMMOTH books, board member of *The Watershed Journal,* and one co-founder of The Watershed Journal Literary Group, which provides publishing opportunities for local writers. Collections include *The Blackbird's Applause, Grass Saxophones, Golden Carp,* and *Chinese Bats.* Forthcoming are *American Zen* and *Blackberry Alleys: Collected Poems and Prose.*

Andrew Vogel

Andrew Vogel teaches at a regional state university in Pennsylvania. His poems have appeared in issues of *The Blue Collar Review, The Heartland Review, Off the Coast, Slant Poetry Journal, The Evergreen Review, The Listening Eye, Plainsongs, The Connecticut River Review, California Quarterly, The Briar Cliff Review, Tule Review,* and elsewhere.

Randi Ward

Randi Ward is a poet, translator, lyricist, and photographer from West Virginia. She earned her MA in Cultural Studies from the University of the Faroe Islands and is a recipient of the American-Scandinavian Foundation's Nadia Christensen Prize. MadHat Press published Ward's second full-length poetry collection, *Whipstitches,* in 2016. For more information, visit www.randiward.com

Jerry Wemple

Pennsylvania native Jerry Wemple is the author of four poetry collections including *You Can See It from Here,* winner of the Naomi Long Madgett Poetry Award. His latest collection, *Artemas and Ark: the Ridge and Valley Poems,* is forthcoming from Finishing Line Press. His creative nonfiction has appeared in *Ninth Letter, Ozy.com* and other venues. He teaches at Bloomsburg University.

Caroline Wermuth

Caroline Wermuth works for the Penn State University Libraries as Outreach Coordinator for the Pennsylvania Center for the Book, where she coordinates the Public Poetry Project, the Lee Bennett Hopkins Award for Children's Poetry, and the Lynd Ward Prize for Graphic Novel. She enjoys writing poems about beautiful natural areas in Pennsylvania.

Karen J. Weyant

Karen J. Weyant's poems and essays have appeared in The Briar Cliff Review, Chautauqua, cream city review, Copper Nickel, Fourth River, Harpur Palate, Lake Effect, Poetry East, Punctuate, Spillway, Stoneboat, Storm Cellar, Waccamaw, and Whiskey Island. She is the author of two poetry chapbooks, Stealing Dust (Finishing Line Press, 2009) and Wearing Heels in the Rust Belt (Winner of Main Street Rag's 2011 Chapbook Contest). She teaches at Jamestown Community College in Jamestown, New York. When she is not teaching, she explores the rural Rust Belt of northern Pennsylvania and western New York.

Rondalyn Whitney

Rondalyn Whitney grew up in rural West Virginia, passionate about writing. She studied journalism, and published several poems, including *Birth Angel* in Yankee Magazine. Dr. Whitney is now a pediatric occupational therapist and professor at WVU, once again living in West Virginia. She is the author of several parenting books, many scholarly works related to public health, as well as non-scholarly articles for the general public.